I Told You So!

Mr. H. G. Wells foreseeing things.

Max

I Told You So!

A Life of H. G. Wells
by James Playsted Wood

Illustrated with Photographs

Pantheon Books

for Bet

I Told You So!

1

Alexander the Great was ambitious. To his ultimate discomfiture so was Julius Caesar.

Most men have their ambitions. Some strive for wealth or fame or both. Some strain only for more impressive homes, more expensive cars, and the envy of their associates; or fatter pensions, more paid holidays, and fringier fringe benefits. A few—it is harder to obtain—struggle to gain their own approval.

Herbert George Wells had larger ambitions than any of these.

Five feet five inches tall, round, with bright blue eyes in a small round head and an urgent high-pitched voice, he wanted to remake the world which Caesar and Alexander had sought merely to conquer. His ambition was to shape and form the economic, social, and political world of his own and all future time and the lives and thoughts of all the people in it. Charged with tremendous energy and a formidable self-assurance, impatient, belligerent, and insistently vocal, he spent most of his life trying to do it.

Long before there were man-made, man-carrying satellites he sped through space, circled the stars, and explored the moon. He foretold the Martian invasion of the planet Earth, which—with a little help from radio and Orson Welles—panic-stricken thousands believed was taking place on the night of October 30, 1938.

H. G. Wells traveled backward and forward in time as he wished. He made a man invisible. Thirty-one years before it was dropped on Hiroshima he predicted the atom bomb. He rewrote the world's history as he thought it should be written and outlined the world's future as he demanded it be lived.

H. G. Wells was a journalist, which is what, accurately, he called himself. He was a novelist. He was (sometimes) a humorist. He was a popularizer. He was a teacher, a seer, a socialist, a prophet, a reformer, a world planner, an unsuccessful labor politician, a pamphleteer, and a public figure on two continents. He was something of a scientist, something of a sociologist, something of a political scientist, and everything of a propagandist. H. G. Wells was irrepressible, indefatigable, and by most ordinary standards illimitable.

Wells might never have decided to remake the world if he had liked the one into which he was born. He did not.

H. G. Wells was born in Bromley, Kent, a London suburb, September 21, 1866. His father, son of the gardener to Lord de Lisle at Penhurst Place in Kent, had been first a gardener himself and was now an unsuccessful shopkeeper and a successful professional athlete, a cricketer. Wells's mother had been a lady's maid.

Wells was born over the glass and china shop which his

Sarah Wells

Joseph Wells

father had purchased from a cousin. Another cousin owned a nearby grocery. For Wells's father, Joseph Wells, shopkeeping was a step up from being a gardener. He was an entrepreneur and his own master. To have risen from the servant to the shopkeeping class was a step up for Wells's mother too, and Sarah Wells was determined that she and her family retain the comparative social eminence which they had achieved.

When he was born, H. G. Wells had two brothers, Frank, who was nine years old, and Fred, four. Undersized and active, bright from the beginning, "Bert" was the spoiled and petted baby of the family, highly vocal and determined on having his own way. A conventionally devout member of the Church of England, Sarah Wells insisted on the gentility she had learned to admire as a lady's maid. Muscular and well-coordinated, Joseph Wells talked loudly and briskly to his fellow shopkeepers as he swept the sidewalk in front of his shop in the mornings. He was also a reader. There were books in the living quarters over the shop, and Joseph Wells brought books home continually. Reading was a family habit.

The shop itself was not central to the life of Wells's father. Cricket was his real life. He coached young men at the Bromley Cricket Club in which he was a leading figure. He played professionally for various clubs and finally played county cricket for Kent itself. In the busy and fast-growing suburb of Bromley he was accorded the respect and admiration that a member of the Boston Red Sox or the Washington Redskins might have in the United States today.

Though his was supposedly a crockery shop, he made Atlas House, as it was called, more of a sporting-goods store instead. He stocked and sold cricket balls, bats, pads, and other paraphernalia of the game, advertising his wares in the local newspapers. He got the balls and bats from still another cousin who manufactured them. Mostly he got them free. He had once saved a member of his cousin's family from drowning, and they were grateful.

Sent first to a dame school to learn his letters, Wells was enrolled in Bromley Academy with his brothers. His mother wanted her sons to have what she considered the intellectual and social advantages of private school education. According to Wells the advantages were few. The academy's master and proprietor kept order with cane and ruler but taught practically nothing. Wells, who later made ferocious attacks on inefficient education a hallmark of his work, drew on memories of Bromley Academy for passages in a number of his novels. His stalwart older brothers, particularly the inventive and restless Frank, were leaders in school pranks. By contrast, Bert Wells was known as a "mama's boy." Small, bookish, already gifted at humorous sketching, he learned much more than he was taught.

A broken leg helped. Wells often called it the most fortunate accident of his life. On the cricket field a friendly young man tossed the small boy good-naturedly in the air, then flubbed his catch. H. G. Wells and the world collided hard for the first time, and the world won. Wells was carted home. His leg was set, and he was en-throned on the parlor sofa where he became the center of household and neighborhood attention. The remorseful mother of his unintentional assailant sent him jams, jellies, and other delicacies. Wells's father brought him books.

His active imagination fired by the enforced inactivity, Wells applied his newly learned skill of reading to illustrated books of geography and natural history. There was a set of Washington Irving at home, so he learned of Spain and Columbus and the American West. In his *Experiment in Autobiography* Wells says he did not remember reading stories or novels at the time. It was later that he came to the popular boys' books and read James Fenimore Cooper and Mayne Reid. He never became addicted to novel-reading for pleasure. Even as a small boy Wells was too intent and intense for that.

A second broken leg a few years later had an even more decisive effect on his life.

This time the broken leg was his father's. One Sunday morning in 1877 while Wells, now eleven years old, and his mother were at church, Joseph Wells propped up a ladder unsteadily to trim a grapevine in the garden behind Atlas House. The ladder gave way. Wells and his mother returned from church to find him groaning on the ground with a compound fracture of the thigh. As he was to use so much of his life in his stories, Wells used this incident in *The New Machiavelli*.

This broken leg was no good fortune. It was a disaster for Joseph Wells and all his family. It was the end of his career in cricket. The shop had never supported the family which now lost its main source of income. For a time

H. G. Wells at about age ten.

they struggled on as best they could, but the neglected Atlas House—marked by a figure of Atlas holding up the world—could not hold them up. Decisive changes had to be made.

The once young woman whom proper Sarah Wells had served was now mistress of a large country estate, Up Park. Mistress and maid had maintained friendly relations. Mrs. Wells appealed to her at a time when Miss Fetherstonhaugh needed domestic help. The result was that Sarah Wells returned happily to service, but this time to the fairly exalted position of housekeeper in an establishment with many servants. Lamed Joseph Wells stayed on in his shop where, in all, he spent thirty years. The oldest son, Frank, had finished his apprenticeship and now had a job as a draper. Fred had almost finished his apprenticeship in the same trade. It was now Bert's turn to go out into the world, and it was his mother's wish that he enter what she saw as the genteel and very respectable business of being a draper.

A draper is a retail dealer in cloth or an employee in such a shop, a clerk in a dry-goods store. In a day when less was ready-made and more sewing of dresses, underclothing, shirts, curtains, sheets—of most of the textiles that people wear or use in their houses—was done at home, the dry-goods store was an important retail outlet. People bought yard goods of wool, cotton, silk, satin, linen, gingham from obsequious and gentlemanly clerks. The drapers and their assistants displayed bolts of cloth for the inspection and approval of their customers, measured off the selected materials, wrapped them, and might even carry them to the customer's waiting carriage.

Just as other boys were apprenticed as carpenters and joiners or as printers or butchers, boys in their early teens were apprenticed to drapers to learn the trade. Their business was to fetch and carry, to run errands, to fold up bolts tumbled in disarray as customers made their choice, and to replace them on the shelves. They swept, dusted, scrubbed, and helped with the window displays. They were taught to be polite, even to be subservient, and to dress with black jacket, cravat, and wing-collar decorum. Frank and Fred Wells had been able to live at home during their apprenticeships. There was no real Wells home now. Apprentices and junior clerks who could not live at home lived in dormitories provided by their masters, ate the food which was generally as bleak as their quarters, and somehow got along with little or no money.

Under his mother's guidance Herbert George Wells was duly and dutifully apprenticed to a draper in Windsor. He was thirteen years old and probably as miserable as any other thirteen-year-old boy sent away to school or into some strange environment by himself for the first time. He was puny, undersized, and clever. He knew a little geography, a little French, a little mathematics, and rather something more of bookkeeping which was a specialty at the Bromley Academy. He had been petted at home but had learned to fend for himself at school. He had the Cockney's resilience and suspiciousness.

Technically, a Cockney is someone born within the sound of the bells of St. Mary-le-Bow Church in East London, and Wells was a suburbanite, but he had the inborn characteristics of the Cockney. He was quick-witted, irreverent, hostile to pretentiousness or to anything he did not understand. He was good humored but always ready to take offense. He was a Cockney, and he was, then and later, cocky.

At school his quickness had let him outdistance his fellows with little effort. His mind and imagination overflowed with all he had read. He was the hero of all the adventure on the Great Plains or in the Rocky Mountains that he knew. He was the victorious general in all the military campaigns he had read about. In spirit he was ruthless, cunning, sage, and glorious—certainly not the rabbitlike ribbon clerk he felt he was expected to become.

Wells did not merely dislike being a draper's apprentice. He hated it. He was deliberately uninterested and naturally clumsy. He could do little right, and he made no effort to do what he knew was demanded of him. His tactics and his general ineptitude worked. His trial apprenticeship with Messrs. Rogers and Denyer opposite the castle in Windsor was soon ended. Wells was dismissed as untidy and troublesome and went happily back to his mother at Up Park. Up Park was the country. It was spaciousness and leisure. Not too far away were girl cousins, laughter and music. He spent as much time with these cousins as he could.

A little upset, Sarah Wells cast about for some new place for her youngest son. She found one. A one-armed uncle had started a school in Wookey in Somersetshire. Wells was sent there to become pupil-teacher under an energetic and individualistic schoolmaster. The uncle had taught school for a time in the West Indies and was afire

with new ideas. In less than three months it was discovered that he did not possess the certificates necessary
to teach in England. The school was closed, and Wells
was soon back again at Up Park.

Brought up over a shop on High Street, Bromley, Wells
found Up Park a revelation. This was the English country
house. The family and their guests were gentry. His
mother ranked high in the hierarchy of the servant staff,
and Miss Fetherstonhaugh was kind to her housekeeper's
son. He had the run of the estate, of the servants' quarters, and of the Up Park library. Well fed, at leisure and
at ease, Wells would willingly have stayed on reading
and sketching for a long time at Up Park. He produced
a daily newspaper, gave a shadow play for the servants,
read, and reveled in the large rooms, the dignity, and the
culture of generations manifested in furniture and curios
accumulated over the years. Throughout life Wells admired the degree of civilization attained in the English
country house, but he was not allowed to linger. His
mother was growing more and more anxious for him to
get started in the world.

Sarah Wells took him to Midhurst, Sussex, where she
had been born and where Wells's maternal grandparents
had kept an inn. At Midhurst she apprenticed him to a
pharmaceutical chemist named Samuel Evan Cowap.
Wells liked pretty Midhurst. He liked the attractive little
drugstore. He liked being where his grandfather and
grandmother had lived. The trouble was that H. G. Wells,
now fifteen, did not want to be a druggist any more than
he wanted to be a draper.

He washed bottles, swept the floor, minded store,

romped with other apprentices, and began to study Latin. A druggist had to know Latin in order to read prescriptions so he was sent to Horace Byatt, headmaster of the Midhurst Grammar School. Wells liked Latin, which seemed to him then the key to all the world of learning he had been shut out from by his servitude to forced labor, and astounded Byatt by his rapid progress. He bided his time with Cowap but not for long. He pointed out to his mother that the money needed to train him fully as a druggist was beyond her means, and this apprenticeship, too, ended.

Until she could find another place to put him, Sarah Wells entered her son as the only boarder at the newly reopened Midhurst Grammar School. This suited Wells fine, but in April 1881 he was placed on trial again as an apprentice draper, this time, at the advice of Miss Fetherstonhaugh's agent, with Edwin Hyde, proprietor of an emporium in Southsea, a prosperous shore resort.

In two novels, *Kipps* and *The History of Mr. Polly*, Wells has left detailed pictures of his days as a draper's apprentice. The novels are light and humorous, two of the pleasantest that Wells wrote. The actuality was different. For two years Wells managed to endure what he continued to detest. He spent every weekend in the luxury of Up Park with his mother or—with them paying his railroad fare—with one or another of his draper brothers, but he spent the days between in bitter complaint or sullen resentment.

He continued to read everything that interested him, and almost everything did, but he continued to hate his life. He found it almost impossible to endure the dull routine, the orders of superiors whom he considered ignorant, and the subservience demanded by his position. Undersized and astigmatic, he could not learn to handle the bolts of cloth with anything approaching expertness, and he did not wish to. He was hotly indignant at the role into which life had thrust him. It might do for others, for millions of others, but not for H. G. Wells.

Many men have suffered real hardships in childhood and youth. Wells did not. Many have survived physical, social, financial, and other assorted handicaps. They have managed to overcome them, tried to forget them, and gone on to success, failure, or indifference. H. G. Wells was not one of them. To the end of his long life he was bitter about what he saw as the unfair disadvantages of his birth, upbringing, and early experiences in the ordinary business of trying to get started making a living.

Wells felt that he had been singled out for abuse and that the working experience of his teens degraded and damaged him. Wells's social consciousness was sharpened by his few brief years as an unwilling apprentice to a trade he detested. He would have detested any trade.

He knew that he was mentally alert and probably superior to many of his fellows. He had done well enough at school in Bromley. At Midhurst he had raced through some elementary mathematical and scientific textbooks with ease. He felt denied, hunted, and humiliated by working thirteen hours a day at the peremptory beck and impatient call of the Southsea drapers whom he detested.

His mother had already paid out forty pounds, a considerable sum of money in the 1880s—about five hundred dollars in terms of today's purchasing power—as a premium for his training. She was liable for ten more pounds. Sarah Wells pleaded with her son to be patient and endure. Her small, thin, angry-eyed son ranted and threatened.

A chance at salvation came when Horace Byatt offered him a post as student assistant in the Midhurst Grammar School at a salary of twenty pounds the first year, forty the second.

Wells was legally and morally bound by his indentures. His mother was liable for the contract she had assumed. Despite all this, Wells, aged seventeen, decided to take a chance and damn the consequences. Writing many years after the event, and with hindthought to straighten out the confusion of his emotions at a time of crisis, he said he made it a guiding point from then on to change his life when he did not like it.

His actual escape was melodramatic. Twenty-six years later Wells reported it almost factually in *Tono-Bungay*. One Sunday morning he bolted Hyde's and Southsea and went back to home and mother. Walking the ten or twelve miles—he says seventeen in his autobiography—back to Up Park, he arrived just as the procession of servants was returning from church. He called out gaily to his mother. Then he told her fiercely that if his apprenticeship articles were not canceled he would drown himself.

Sarah Wells did not wish him to drown himself. Neither was H. G. Wells insistent on drowning. What he really wanted was escape from durance vile. He escaped, and life never captured H. G. Wells again. It was much more nearly—as much more nearly as Wells could make it in long years of hard trying—the other way around.

2

Student Assistant Herbert George Wells, late apprentice draper in Windsor and Southsea and apprentice chemist to Samuel Cowap, worked ecstatically under Horace Byatt, M.A., in the Midhurst Grammar School. He had got home to the grandparental village. There were pleasant walks and glorious talks. He had got home to a life he liked among people he liked and respected. Fired with new zeal, he set himself demanding tasks and thrilled to performing them.

Under Byatt's direction he taught small boys firmly and forcefully. Because it was obligatory and despite the atheism which he had adopted and of which he was proud, he joined the Church of England. He refused to read plays or light novels. Only non-fiction of substance would satisfy his desire and his ambitions. He surged ahead with determination and intent.

He shone in the role for which Byatt had really selected him. Wells was quick to grasp outlines, able to sort out and absorb masses of new facts. He had demonstrated this earlier to the surprised schoolmaster. Byatt had his

assistant put this ability and his facility at passing examinations to good use for both of them.

The Education Board empowered Byatt to teach evening classes in some thirty different subjects. He taught
some of them and was paid in grants when his students
passed their final examinations. Wells passed many for
him. He also passed a number which Byatt did not teach
and in which there were no actual classes. Byatt simply
obtained the textbooks. Wells raced through them, boned
up on the subjects, and passed the examinations for which
he received educational credits, and Byatt the additional
income.

Wells responded to the thrills of success and reward
after effort. He drove at his studies. He passed examinations in elementary physiography, geology, mathematics,
and chemistry. He studied outlines of physics and biology. He had something to boast about when he returned
to Up Park for his holidays, danced at a party for all the
servants, and had an enjoyable flirtation with one of the
housemaids.

Back at Midhurst he read books on economics as well
as science. He stumbled upon a classic in political science.
One of the books he read was Plato's *Republic*. Another
was *Progress and Poverty* by Henry George. These were
key books in helping to form the utopian and socialistic
ideas which began to glimmer in Wells's mind.

Wells was elated. His world was widening unbeliev-
ably. Soon he knew even greater elation. The Education
Board sent out circulars to successful examinees in various
subjects offering teacher-in-training scholarships at the

Normal School of Science in London. In effect what Wells had done was to pass the entrance examinations for a normal school, or as they are now called, a teachers' college.

Wells applied for one of the advertised scholarships. His application was approved. Suddenly he possessed a scholarship worth a guinea a week—say twenty to twenty-five dollars—his railway fare to London, and free tuition for a year. Hugging himself with excitement and eager anticipation, Wells spent his summer holidays at Up Park and made a visit to his lame and lonely father at Atlas House. Then in 1884, when he was eighteen years old, he descended on London as a normal-school student. As great a thrill for Wells as this triumph was the knowledge that Thomas Henry Huxley was to be one of his instructors. To Wells, Huxley was godlike. For the rest of his life he referred to Huxley as the greatest man he ever knew.

Charles Darwin had published his *Origin of Species* in 1859. This was the great work which introduced the theory of biological evolution. The *Origin of Species* shook the scientific world and threw the theological into agonies of recrimination and denial. Science received the new doctrine with rapt enthusiasm. The church condemned it. The idea that man was descended from lower life forms horrified all those who had been taught and had believed that man had been made in the image of God. Science had a different conception of God, or like the youthful H. G. Wells, none at all and no interest in having any. Suddenly science was all the rage. Science would accomplish miracle on miracle. Completely unscientific people were rapturous about it, and H. G. Wells was more rapturous than most.

Darwin introduced the theory of evolution, but its great popularizer was Thomas Henry Huxley. Born in 1825, Huxley had been a doctor in the Royal Navy. He became interested in marine life, published a number of papers on it, and became a naturalist in the Geological Survey and a lecturer on natural history at the Royal School of Mines. Attracted by ideas of organic evolution, he immediately adopted Darwinism, defended it, lectured about it, wrote about it, and taught it. Eminent and highly respected, Huxley was the foremost exponent of biological evolution in England.

Wells did not study science with the idea of making it his profession. He took courses given to acquaint student teachers with what they would need to know in order to teach at an elementary or secondary school level. During his first year he had elementary biology and then zoölogy under Huxley. Huxley he worshipped. G. B. Howes, who taught while Huxley was ill, he admired. Wells worked hard in the laboratory on the top floor of the red brick and stucco Normal School of Science that first year, and he did well in his examinations.

He did less well his second year. He knew his way around, and had got over his awe. He mingled freely with fellow students among whom his irreverence and cockney sharpness gave him a reputation as a wit. He played the role to the hilt and enjoyed it. He was disputative and amusing, and he knew it. He became active in the student debating society.

With his fellows Wells visited the museums in London, the art galleries, and the libraries. They were free. He began to read books like Carlyle's *French Revolution* for their thought-provoking pleasure rather than for their practical use in passing examinations. During his second year Wells decided that the quality of teaching at the Normal School was poor. As much as he dared he became derisive in class. He was not a good laboratory worker, but as Wells was often wont to do, he turned this failing into a virtue by burlesquing the work. At the end of the year Wells did badly in his final examinations.

Other things were attracting his critical attention. He saw the wealth and ease in London. He also saw the slums and poverty. He heard George Bernard Shaw—whom he distrusted from the first—speak at a meeting of the Fabian Society. The society had been founded as a socialistic organization in 1884. Shaw was too flippant for Wells's taste. He took socialism more seriously and became an avowed socialist and revolutionist.

The nineteen-year-old wit, iconoclast, atheist, and socialist found other distractions.

On first coming to London he had lodged in a small, very crowded house in Westbourne Park, a place his always solicitous mother had found for him. Two families with their children lived in the house, and the rest of it was crammed with lodgers. This was coarse, lower-class London. The amusements of his Westbourne Park companions were the music halls, the pubs, Saturday shopping on crowded Edgeware Road, and huge Sunday dinners followed by afternoons of indiscriminate petting. Wells indulged readily in all of these extracurricular activities but found himself shrinking from some aspects of life in the house.

He complained to a woman cousin of his father's. After discreet explanation to his father in Bromley and his mother at Up Park, the cousin, who worked in a fashionable department store, promptly installed Wells with two aunts on his father's side who kept a boarding house on Euston Road in Bloomsbury.

The house was a tall row house. The top floor was let to an aged clergyman and his wife. There was a woman university student and a German woman among the other lodgers. Wells was given his own small room and the privilege of doing his homework in the basement, which was crowded with bookshelves, a piano, a curio stand, and all the ornaments and intricacies of Victorian decoration.

His aunts Mary and Arabella were women much like his mother. They wore caps and small aprons over their dark silk gowns. Wells was happier than he had been, and indeed well off, for all the rest of his student days in London. He was at home, and he had a constant companion in his cousin Isabel, who was his own age. Pretty, grave, gentle, Isabel Mary Wells worked in a photographer's shop on Regent Street. Every morning Wells walked part way to work with her. Every evening he sought her out as soon as he came back from his classes. Before long Wells was passionately in love with his cousin and eager to marry her.

If Wells had done poorly in his second year at the Normal School, he did much worse in his third. He was

restless, dissatisfied, impatient. Afire with ideas, ⸱
ing with energy, he talked excitedly with his fellow
was bored with his teachers and wanted Isabel. He w
brash, ill-mannered, and overexcited. In later life he could
hardly explain these derelictions except to say that part of
it all was innate in his temperament. "I am a typical Cockney without either reverence or a sincere conviction of
inferiority to any fellow creature."

He complained of lack of funds. His weekly guinea suf-
ficed for necessary expenditures but left him little to
spend on diversions. As earlier, he felt unjustly put upon.
Many American students, of necessity, try to "work their
way through" school or college. Wells made no effort to
earn money for himself. He was a student and would have
considered menial work beneath him. He complained
then and later of the deprivations he suffered as a student,
but he blamed the system not himself. Even in the long
vacations he did not work. He took his holidays as a
gentleman of leisure at Up Park. In the summer of 1886,
when he was twenty years old, he stayed on the Glouces-
tershire farm of an uncle, making excursions from
there to delightful Cheltenham Spa, a famed resort, and
to the ancient Royal Forest of Dean.

When he took his examinations at the end of his third
year, Wells failed completely in astronomical physics. He
did badly in elementary physics and in geometry. He
failed more subjects, scraped by in others. The results of
all the distractions and his inability to concentrate on
detailed work were inevitable. Wells knew that he was "a
candidate for expulsion," and he was even then an ac-

curate prophet. His scholarship was not renewed.

The aspiring teacher was nearly twenty-one years old. He had to look for a teaching position with no college degree and somewhat less than a mediocre normal-school record behind him. His appearance was not more pre-possessing than his credentials. He was short, untidy, and meager. He weighed only about one hundred and fifteen pounds. He was already uneasy with the journalistic am-bitions which had led him to help establish and write for the *Science School Journal.* He was abrim with socialistic ideas. He was engaged to marry his cousin Isabel but was without the financial prospects which would make mar-riage possible.

Through an agency he managed to get hired as a teacher in a private school in Wales. It was a poor school crudely operated by an incompetent headmaster. Wells did not like the school or the people in it, but there were compensations. He flirted pleasantly with a high school teacher on vacation. While the weather was good he en-joyed the countryside about Wrexham. Soon he was to leave Holt Academy in worse straits than he had arrived.

No athlete, he was badly hurt trying to play football with the students. A crushed left kidney caused internal bleeding. While he was recovering as best he could in bleak surroundings with little attention, he began hemor-rhaging from the lungs. A local physician diagnosed tu-berculosis.

Wells retreated once more to his mother at Up Park, where he was installed in a warm and sunny room. The brilliant young Dr. William Job Collins happened to be a guest at the country house at the time. He attended Wells and verified the Wrexham physician's diagnosis. Wells was tubercular. His right lung had been affected. Dr. Collins did not see it as a terminal or even very serious case. He felt that after a year or so of rest and restrained activity his patient would fully recover. He feared that the crushed kidney would cause trouble later and that Wells might become diabetic. For the time being he prescribed complete rest.

This time Wells played the gay invalid with zest during his months at Up Park. Though he fretted a little at the interruption of a career that had not yet started and seemed as if it might never start, he wrote facetious letters to friends and enjoyed his comfortable surroundings. This was almost as good as the broken leg he had suffered as a child. He started, but did not finish, writing a novel.

His father's business had finally failed in Bromley. The shop had been sold out from under him, and his father was living on an allowance from his wife in a cottage about three miles from Up Park. Wells's oldest brother, Frank, gave up the drapery business he had never liked and joined their father. He proposed to make his living selling and repairing clocks and watches. The other brother, Fred, joined them all at Christmas for the holiday dinner in the servants' hall at Up Park.

Rampant socialist that he had become, and unconventional as he prided himself upon being in other ways, Wells was always conventional and practical enough where his ambitions were concerned.

From Up Park he wrote a long and pretentiously stilted

young man's letter to Dr. Collins soliciting his aid as a patron. He reminded the doctor that men like Thomas Henry Huxley and George Bernard Shaw had to have secretaries and assistants. He asked Dr. Collins, who he knew was well connected, to help him get such a post. Dr. Collins sympathized but said he was unable to forward his impatient patient's ambitions in that direction.

It was the summer of 1888, a year after he had gone to teach at Holt, before Wells was well enough to leave Up Park to stay with friends in Stoke on Trent. From there he returned to London where he was able to obtain some tutoring work. Early the following year his luck improved. Wells was hired as an assistant master in the Henley House school of John Vine Milne. The headmaster was the father of A. A. Milne, then a small boy. He is thus the grandfather of Winnie-the-Pooh.

This was Wells's first real teaching job and for the time, the place, and the young teacher it was a good one. J. V. Milne was a sound and forward-looking headmaster. He was both a capable teacher and in theory and practice a liberal educator. Under him Wells got an encouraging start in what for the next half-dozen years would be his profession as a secondary-school teacher.

Milne paid generously. Wells received two pounds a week for teaching science and mathematics. Even he admitted that it was a good salary at the time. Mrs. Milne fed him well. Henley House provided polite and pleasant society. Here he first met Alfred Harmsworth when he returned as an "old boy." Harmsworth, who became Lord Northcliffe, had founded and edited the *Henley House*

Magazine. He became the most powerful newspaper publisher in England.

Encouraged by his happier situation, Wells began adding to his income by teaching physiology and mathematics at a nearby girls' school. He also began to study for qualifying examinations which would give him a Bachelor of Science degree at London University. It was not science but education he studied now, courses in teaching methods and in the elementary subjects he would be licensed to teach. This time and in these subjects he did well. Not only did he pass examinations in the theory and practice of education, geography, arithmetic, drawing, and natural science, but he also won three cash prizes.

As a reward for this achievement and as an inducement for him to stay, Milne raised Wells's salary by ten pounds a year and gave him more free time. Wells contributed to the *Henley House Magazine* and tried to do other writing to add to his income. His attempts came to nothing. No one would buy what he wrote. Then Wells found a better way to earn more money.

He applied for work to William Briggs who had founded a University Correspondence College in Cambridge. Immediately Briggs put Wells to work teaching biology by correspondence at two pounds a week. He further agreed that if Wells took his B.S. degree he would hire him for the staff of a Tutorial College he planned to institute in London. Wells's wages would depend on what honors he took in his examination. For advertising purposes Briggs needed high honors men on his list of tutors.

Wells had incentive now. He wanted as much money as

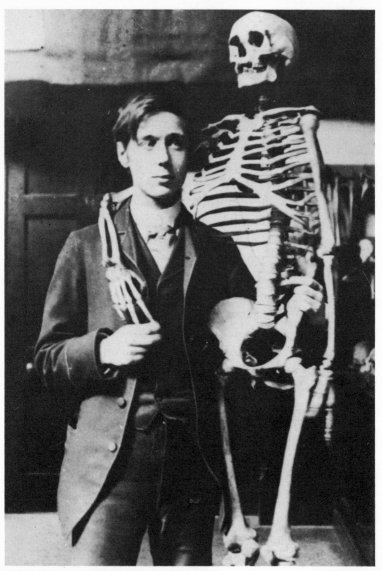

H. G. Wells and friend.

he could earn so that he could marry. He studied hard, polished his old skill at taking examinations, and took his undergraduate degree from London University in October 1890 with first-class honors in zoölogy and second-class in geology. This assured him thirty hours teaching a week at two shillings and four or sixpence an hour in Briggs's Tutorial College.

The concentrated effort had tired H. G. Wells. Dr. Collins sent him back to Up Park for a month's rest. When he returned to London, Wells, who had resigned from Henley House, moved with his fiancée-cousin and her mother to a rented eight-room house in Wandsworth, opened a bank account with money from Milne and Briggs, and began to teach in the Tutorial College, which was at first a room over a bookshop, then a classroom and laboratory in a building in Red Lion Square. In the Wandsworth church, October 31, 1891, Herbert George Wells, aged twenty-five years and one month, and Isabel Mary Wells were married.

The Tutorial College was really a cram school. Wells and a score of other tutors who worked for William Briggs were coaching pupils to pass examinations, particularly the entrance examinations of London University. Briggs himself was adept at passing written tests. Wells could grasp the outlines of a formalized subject with comparative ease, seize on the salient facts, and put them down to the satisfaction of examiners. Under Briggs, Wells used this asset happily and profitably. He taught evening classes. He did some private tutoring. He edited the magazine of the University Correspondence College.

Teaching methodology was his subject now. Beginning more and more to think of himself as a teacher and journalist, Wells wrote articles about teaching for the magazine, reviewed educational textbooks, and finally wrote a *Textbook of Biology* and collaborated with another tutor on another cram text. All of this work was for Briggs who paid Wells for his writing, as for his teaching, at so much an hour.

Stimulated, Wells was burning his abundant energy at a great rate. From his text collaborator, Walter Low, he learned how to go about writing and selling occasional pieces to the London newspapers. He looked enviously at all the signs of prosperity about him and determined to grasp as much as he could for himself.

Wells worked the harder, perhaps, because the marriage to which he had looked forward so intently for almost six years was not working out as he had hoped. It was to have been the culmination of his fierce desire, and he had envisioned exciting bliss. He found that his cousin could not respond with the same ardor that fired him, and that she was immune to the ideas which excited him. Wells was dissatisfied and disappointed.

He drove at his teaching and writing. Experience with minor educational journalism gave him confidence. He found out how to appeal to editors and their readers. He got his first magazine article, "The Rediscovery of the Unique," into the *Fortnightly Review*, edited then by the spectacular Frank Harris, and some scientific pieces into the *Gentleman's Magazine*, for which Dr. Samuel Johnson had written regularly one hundred and fifty years earlier. He got some articles into the London *Globe*.

He also fell in love. Amy Catherine Robbins came as a student to his afternoon class in the Tutorial College at the opening of the 1892–1893 academic year. She was pretty, with fair hair and brown eyes. She was intellectually alert. Quickly student and instructor were friends. Wells lent her books. There were walks and talks, notes. Occasionally the two managed to have tea together. Wells described what must have been something much like their early relationship in *Ann Veronica* in 1909.

It was all too much and too much at once for H. G. Wells. He had tasted success and wanted more of it. He had no doubts about his capabilities. Emotionally he was fretful and perplexed. One night as he was hurrying for the Charing Cross underground station after tutoring a student in geology until nine or ten o'clock he collapsed. In a car of the underground train he used his handkerchief to stanch the bright blood that welled up from his infected lung. Somehow he managed to get home. During the night he suffered more violent hemorrhaging. His wife, his aunt, and a doctor labored over him applying ice bags to stop the bleeding. Wells believed he very nearly died that night in May 1893.

It was the end of his three years in the tutorial college. It was the end, and he knew it at the time, of his teaching career. He had collapsed and so had his family. Never efficient and grown inconveniently deaf, his mother was at odds with her indulgent employer, who had also grown old and whose patience had given out. Sarah Wells was dismissed from her Up Park sinecure. Joseph Wells was living out his years in the cottage with Frank. Fred lost his job as a draper's assistant to the son of his employer. Convalescent once more, Wells urged him to accept the offer of a drapery job in South Africa. Reluctantly, Fred agreed and left England.

Fortunately, Wells had about enough money in the bank to cover expenses for a year or so. He continued his correspondence-course teaching, but that was all he felt he could do. He began to write a geography text for Briggs but never finished it. With his wife and mother-in-law he went off for a two-week holiday to Eastbourne, a popular shore resort on the English Channel.

At Eastbourne he chanced to read *When a Man's Single* by James M. Barrie. Though Barrie had not yet written *Peter Pan* and some of his other successful plays, he was already well known and widely read. From this book of Barrie's, Wells learned a useful secret. The secret was how to write light, bright—and salable—journalistic trifles about almost anything. The trick was to take some commonplace incident, dramatize it a little, and send it to the less demanding newspapers and magazines instead of to the literary periodicals Wells had been attempting to reach.

Wells already knew something of the technique. His writing for Briggs had been largely of this facile and superficial kind. He combined his experience and the Barrie approach. He became a free-lance journalist, but in the larger sense, Wells never ceased to be a teacher. His didacticism was ingrained. He simply left the classroom, became a writer, and starting with the bits and sketches for which he found a ready market, went on to teach on a much larger scale.

3

Wells's success as a contributor to newspapers and magazines was immediate. He had always been articulate. He could write as confidently and vividly as he talked. He could produce in quantity whatever he thought he could sell, and he worked in a seller's market.

Journalism flourished in London in the 1890s. Lacking radio or television, people read for entertainment and information. Vigorous newspaper and magazine editors competed for new contributors whose writing would attract and hold readers. There were many publications, and more came. Just as Wells started on his new profession the opportunities expanded. William Waldorf Astor, grandson of John Jacob Astor, tired of the United States and in 1890 moved to England.

A writer as well as a politician with social ambitions, Astor was above all a capitalist. He was said to have a hundred million dollars, was obviously anxious to spend some of it, and found editors and writers who were very glad to help him do it. In 1893 Astor bought the *Pall Mall Gazette*, a daily newspaper, and its weekly edition, the

Pall Mall Budget. He changed them from liberal to conservative papers and installed Harry Cust, heir to an earldom, as editor.

Well-connected in the world of fashion, Cust was a friend of the redoubtable William Ernest Henley, poet, critic, the sometimes friend and literary adviser of Robert Louis Stevenson, and editor at various times of the *Magazine of Art*, the *National Observer*, and the *New Review*.

To expand his publishing interests Astor established the *Pall Mall Magazine*. Wells wrote the gist of an article about his two-week stay in Eastbourne on the back of an envelope. He lengthened it, gave it "Staying at the Seaside" as title, had it typed by a cousin, and sent it to this newest of the Astor publications. Acceptance was by return mail. Wells wrote another piece and sent it in. It was accepted. He dug up a facetious sketch he had written for the *Science School Journal* while he was a student, rewrote it and submitted it. It was bought for the *Pall Mall Budget*.

Barrie, who had started it all for Wells and was soon his friend, read and liked one of these early Wells contributions and said so. The comic magazine *Punch* noticed one favorably. Wells asked Harry Cust for regular work reviewing books and got it. Other editors wrote the new writer asking for contributions.

There was never a setback. Wells's experience, his cockney shrewdness, his conceit, and his natural expressiveness crystallized in article after article. Quickly he was earning more with his pen—it *was* actually a pen or pencil, for Wells wrote always in longhand, others doing his typing—than he had earned at teaching. His success mounted, and Wells pressed on from mere acceptance to victory and popular triumph.

He solved another problem in 1893. As far back as his flight from Southsea via Up Park to the Midhurst Grammar School he had resolved to change his life when it did not please him. His marriage did not please him. He arranged a divorce from the cousin he had married. They separated before the end of the year, and in January 1894 Wells and Amy Catherine Robbins took lodging together in London. There are reflections of actions, incidents, and what must have been Wells's feelings at the time in *Tono-Bungay*, *Love and Mr. Lewisham*, and in *The New Machiavelli* as well as in *Ann Veronica*.

For some years, like the estranged wife in *Tono-Bungay*, Isabel Wells ran a poultry farm. When she re-married, Wells typically, and despite his earlier dereliction, raged with jealousy. Yet he settled an income on Isabel Wells after he had ceased paying alimony, and at one point when she was gravely ill took her into his own home where he and his second wife helped care for her.

Wells was legally married to his first wife for five years, but the marriage was a reality for little more than three. His second and enduring marriage became a mainstay of his life. He and Amy Catherine Robbins, who was still studying for her B.S. degree when they took up house-keeping, worked together and wandered London together seeking subjects that he could turn into articles and profit. In Amy Catherine Wells, whom he called Jane, he found the compatibility and companionship he had failed to find in his cousin. She ran his home, typed his manuscripts, read the proofs of his books. Though later, as he makes clear, Wells indulged himself in numerous amorous escapades and boasted of himself as a "Don Juan among the intellectuals," he was devoted to her.

Demands for more and longer manuscripts and the stimulus of his new love turned H. G. Wells on several more notches. Some time earlier he had written and rewritten a long story which he called "The Chronic Argonauts." He got it out, swiftly rewrote it, and sold it to Henley's *New Review* as a serial story. *The Time Machine*, as it was retitled, gained wide and favorable attention. It became his first real book.

The accident of timing was as fortunate for H. G. Wells when he began to write books and appear as an author as it had been when he presented himself as a writer of journalistic articles. The giants of English fiction— Dickens, Thackeray, Meredith, Hardy—were either dead or nearing the end of their careers. Most of the new popular writers had come out of the upper or upper-middle classes; Wells came from the lower. They had literary backgrounds, generally in liberal arts, the humanities. They had been drilled in Latin, sometimes Greek, in school and might have read literature and history at Oxford or Cambridge. In contrast, Wells had emerged from a family of shopkeepers and servants. He had no university education. He was contemptuously ignorant of the classical tradition. He had drunk at two welling springs: Science (it almost has to be capitalized in this connotation) and Socialism.

Amy Catherine Wells

He knew something of botany and zoölogy. He was a convinced Darwinist. He had some knowledge of geology and a smattering of physics. Though he was not a dedicated student of any of the scientific disciplines, Science, the idea of Science, fascinated him. It appealed to his imagination. It stimulated his inventiveness. Science was almost his religion.

All this was at a time when science was new to the popular mind. It was new, and it was magic. Science would remake the world. England was coming to the close of a century unrivaled for success and prosperity. It had seen the worldwide triumph of British imperialism and at home economic bliss, through industrialization, for the fortunate. There seemed no reason why this satisfactory state of things should not continue. Progress seemed assured, and Darwinism had shown that biological advance was inevitable. It all went together somehow.

If, for some unlikely reason, science did not save the world, Socialism would. Socialism as well as science was in the air. At the time it was not an actuality, not even a probability, but an almost philanthropic idea among comfortably placed intellectuals. Socialism would abolish all inequities. It would give everybody an equal chance. Scientifically organized, Socialism would transform the social, economic, and political world. Nobody would ever hunger or thirst. Nobody would ever wish to die. Together, Science and Socialism would be irresistible.

H. G. Wells had imbibed both popular ideas early. They became his convictions, and he never changed them. He talked about them, wrote about them, and worked for his conception of their realization. What he first presented in his books was Science.

Wells knew Dickens. Everybody who could read English knew Dickens. Not everybody could write like him. To a certain extent Wells could. He knew Nathaniel Hawthorne, and he was influenced by Hawthorne in his early writing of romance. He also knew Jules Verne whose stories were enormously popular in England. The French writer's *Voyage to the Center of the Earth* had appeared two years before Wells was born, his *Twenty Thousand Leagues Under the Sea* when Wells was three, and his *Around the World in Eighty Days* in 1872 when Wells was six. Verne, who never became a Wells admirer had preceded him. Verne's books, still widely read, are classics of their kind, but Wells, less scientific and more fictional than Verne, is justly regarded as the father of modern science fiction. Had he written nothing else, the series of books, which beginning with *The Time Machine* he wrote in rapid succession, established a reputation which would still stand.

Wells knew London, the suburbs, and the country of the south of England. He knew writers and schoolmasters and science teachers. He knew the surface of ordinary English character. He was extravagantly inventive. He had an assured way with words. He was accustomed to thinking in terms of astronomical space and geological time. He put elements of all this lore together in wild and violent contrast, and breaking down his reader's disbelief by the easy assumption that it was not there, he wrote convincingly of the unknown and unknowable.

Wells fashioned romances of the macabre, the horrible, the fantastic, and the unrealistic in settings which no man had ever seen and presented them as if they were factual incidents, characters, and creatures which no one could disprove. He made his tales exciting, and he made them plausible. Because they grip the imagination and convince the sense, they read as vividly now as when he wrote them.

The Time Machine opens with the Time Traveler (Wells gives him no other name) in conversation with the Provincial Mayor, Filby, who is red-haired and argumentative, a Medical Man, a Very Young Man, and a Psychologist. The host explains to his guests what time really is. In his student days Wells had heard time discussed as the fourth dimension, and it is as the fourth dimension that he has his Time Traveler present it. Every body, he says, must have its existence in four dimensions: length, breadth, thickness, and duration. "There is no difference between Time and any of the three dimensions of Space except that our consciousness moves along it."

The Time Traveler had been at work, and he had perfected a machine in which he could travel back and forth in time just as other machines move about in space. He showed his guests a small model. Wells's description of it is vague. It had parts of ivory and "some crystalline substance." There was a bar which seemed unreal, and there were two levers, one for traveling backward and the other for traveling forward in time. Later he showed them the machine itself and declared his intention of exploring time in it.

A week later the same men, the Narrator and the editor

Blank, returned as his dinner guests. Their host was late. They were about to sit down to dinner without him when he appeared battered, limping, and bleeding. He could tell them nothing until he had drunk champagne and eaten ravenously of meat, good wholesome meat. "I'm starving for a bit of meat!"

Then he told the fantastic tale which the Narrator recorded. Since four o'clock that afternoon the Time Traveler had spent eight days in the far future. He had, in fact, landed in his machine in the year 802,701. He had landed near temple ruins and columns amid the most beautiful creatures he had ever seen. They laughed and danced and sang. The air was perfectly clear. There were no gnats or other insects. There were no animals. Horses, dogs, and cattle were all extinct. People ate only fruit. They did no work. It was, or seemed to be, an Elysium in which the world and its human inhabitants had achieved idyllic perfection.

Then the Time Traveler discovered that these beautiful people were without intellect. They had the minds of five-year-old children. He saw why.

For the first time I began to realize an odd consequence of the social effort in which we are at present engaged. And yet, come to think, it is a logical consequence enough. Strength is the outcome of need: security sets a premium on feebleness. The work of ameliorating the conditions of life—the true civilising process that makes life more and more secure—had gone steadily on to a climax. One triumph of a united humanity over Nature had followed another. Things that are now mere dreams had become projects deliberately in hand and carried forward. And the harvest was what I saw! . . . Humanity had been strong, energetic, and intelligent, and had used all its abundant vitality to alter the conditions under which it lived. . . . Under the new conditions of perfect comfort and security, that restless energy, that with us is strength, would become weakness.

Then the Time Traveler had become aware of ghostly figures with staring eyes who moved only at night. Taken by whom or why he does not know, his Time Machine disappears into the hollow pedestal of the White Sphinx. Clambering fearfully around what seem to be temple ruins, he comes on a shaft which leads underground into a maze of tunnels and caverns.

He heard the hum of machinery. Great creatures with large eyes which could not stand light seized at him in the darkness. He saw them now. They were ". . . nauseatingly inhuman . . . pale, chinless faces and great, lidless, pinkish-grey eyes!"

The beautiful people above ground were the Eloi. These underground horrors were the Morlocks. Another species which had resulted from man's evolution, the Morlocks were the real rulers. They fed and cared for the Eloi—and raised them like cattle for food. The Morlocks came up at night to seize their prey.

The Time Traveler escaped above ground, but at night the Morlocks pursued him and a child-woman of the Eloi whom he had befriended. He managed to get inside the White Sphinx to his machine, which he knew now the Morlocks had set there as bait in a trap. He leaped into the saddle, pulled the return lever, and returned to face his astonished dinner guests.

At the end of his first science-fiction tale Wells says:

> So, as I see it, the Upper-world man had drifted toward his feeble prettiness, and the Under-world to more mechanical industry. . . . Apparently, as time went on, the feeding of the Under-world, . . . had become disjointed. Mother Necessity, who had been staved off for a few thousand years, came back again, and she began below. The Under-world being in contact with machinery . . . had probably retained perforce rather more initiative, if less of every other human character, than the upper. And when other meat failed them, they turned to what old habit had hitherto forbidden.

The Time Machine was a thriller and acclaimed as a thriller. It wrought fascination and an involuntary shudder. Yet it contained much of the essential and lasting Wells: "science," organic evolution, and social advance through concerted effort. The odd thing is—and it contrasts strongly with the bulk of his later work—that it shows Wells pessimistic about the distant results of evolution and social progress. It all ended in weakness, in the ascendancy of the sub-human over the human, and in cannibalism.

Henley paid Wells an enormous one hundred pounds

for *The Time Machine* as a serial. Heinemann brought it out as a book. Wells was made dramatic critic for the *Pall Mall Gazette* and began attending the theater with his fellow critic George Bernard Shaw.

Wells and Amy Catherine Robbins, whom he married as soon as his divorce came through, moved from one place to another in London. They worked hard and they lived merrily. They mingled with the new literary friends and the editors and critics whom Wells' new success brought within their orbit. They enjoyed their domestic jokes, Wells exuberantly sketching what—with the penchant for baby talk that is always disconcerting—he called "picshuas" of their household antics. They moved again, this time to Woking and a small semi-detached villa. There Wells labored fiercely on more science fiction. They bought bicycles and began to explore the countryside on what was then the novel and exhilarating mode of easy and daringly fast locomotion.

In 1896 Wells published *The Island of Dr. Moreau.* The tale is "science," and it is fiction. It is also obscenely gruesome.

Edward Prendick, who tells the story, is picked up unconscious at sea after the sinking of a ship on which he was a passenger. Aboard the rescue ship, captained by a brutal skipper, he finds a Dr. Montgomery, who attends him, a caged puma, llama, rabbits, and a dark, misshapen hairy man of whom the crew and all the animals are afraid. Though Montgomery does not wish to take him, Prendick is forced ashore with the doctor, the animals, and the monster man. They are rowed to an unnamed island by a crew of bandaged and grotesquely shapen oarsmen.

They land on the island of Dr. Moreau, a notorious vivisectionist exiled from England after disclosure of his barbarous experimentation on animals. Prendick tells the white-haired Doctor (Wells, always careless of details, calls him gray-haired later) that "he had spent some years at the Royal College of Science and had done some research in biology under Huxley." In most of his novels and stories Wells managed to use parts of his background of which he was proud as the background of his heroes.

Shut in a locked room, Prendick hears the agonized screaming of the puma. Moreau and Montgomery, a drunkard whom Moreau has given sanctuary from punishment for nameless crimes, are creating men out of beasts by surgical mutilation. The island is peopled with Beast Men. There are Monkey-Men, Leopard-Men, Hyena-Men, Ox-Boar Men, Dog-Men, and others. The animals are butchered in "The House of Pain," then made to live, deformed and distorted, in subservience to Moreau. They are tortured mentally as well as physically. Moreau indoctrinates them psychologically to smother their instincts and to obey his commands.

By accident some of the Beast Men taste blood. They turn on Moreau. The Puma-Man batters in the scientist's head. Montgomery too is killed by the distortions he has helped perpetrate. Prendick is left alone with only Moreau's whip and Montgomery's revolver to quell the Beast Men, who look to him as their new master.

The Beast Men revert to animals, living in their lairs and prowling by night. Prendick finally escapes in a boat which drifts to shore with two dead men in it. The Wolf-Man and the Bear-Man try to drag him back, but after three days at sea he is picked up by a brig and gets back to England.

Prendick recovers somewhat after treatment by "a mental specialist," but terror of the island of Dr. Moreau haunts him.

> My trouble took the strangest form. I could not per-suade myself that the men and women I met were not also another, still passably human, Beast People, animals half-wrought into the outward image of human souls, and that they would presently begin to revert, to show first this bestial mark and then that.

The essential beastliness of the human being is about the only meaning that can be read into what otherwise is merely a shocking and sickening story. Wells saw man as only another of the animals. There was a popular outcry at the time against the vivisection of animals in scientific experiments, and he took advantage of this protest to sell his wares. He carried the real excesses of vivisection to an imagined ultimate.

His science fiction was bringing H. G. Wells money and fame. He mined the vein he had discovered with frenzied energy and firm intent. This exploitation of "science" was establishing him as a successful writer. His stories were not seriously considered to be literary work. They were looked upon as gaudy thrillers, books for boys. Wells resented this, for he wanted to be taken seri-ously, but he was elated at his popularity and determined to capitalize upon it.

His next thriller is perhaps still his best and best known.

When it was first made into a motion picture, it established the reputation of Claude Rains, even though he was never seen on the screen. He was The Invisible Man.

The Invisible Man is more skillfully concocted than Wells's first scientific romances. It is set in familiar quiet English places, the strangeness of the story gaining credence by reader acceptance of the scene and characters, and the fantasy greater force through the chilling contrast of the known with the unknown. Again, Wells is hardly scientific in his science, but that does not seem to matter. It is the incidents and the horror reactions of those involved to the spectral phenomenon in their midst that grip the reader.

Somehow—Wells says by lowering the refractive index of any substance to that of air—a young physicist in London learns how to make himself invisible. An albino in coloring, or lack of it, he first tries his discovery on a dirty white cat, then on himself. He and the cat both disappear from sight. Inability to survive invisible in London, then in the Sussex village of Iping to which he flees, turns Griffin frantic.

For no discernible reason, except perhaps that the Hyde of Jekyll and Hyde was evil, the invisible man is evil. He attacks people without reason. He kills a helpless chief of police. He tries to force a Dr. Kemp, whom he had known in his student days, to become his confederate in a reign of terror. Instead, Griffin is hunted down by a panic-stricken mob and battered to death with clubs and spades. The invisible man becomes visible only as he lies dying in the street.

The point of this fantasy seems to be fantasy merely. Or perhaps the point is that what is different is detestable. Griffin lives these few days in a paroxysm of helplessness. He arouses repugnance and fear, hatred and the compulsion to destroy. The man who is invisible has a hard time of it. So do people who recoil generally at any aberrations from the norm. They seem to be against scientific improvement in the appearance—here the non-appearance —of their kind.

There was consternation and mass fear that night in 1938 when Martians overran northern New Jersey and attacked New York. Obviously the human race, helpless before the onslaught, was coming to a fiery end. Even after they were reassured, many people would not believe that what they had heard was not appalling final fact, but rather a broadcast, with too realistic effect, of H. G. Wells's *The War of the Worlds* rewritten for radio.

Most of the popular ideas of Mars and Martians, the games, toys, and headgear of small boys playing at being space people armed with devastating weapons, come from *The War of the Worlds*. The title is inaccurate. What Wells depicted so vividly in his story of 1898 was the invasion of England by creatures from Mars.

A great incandescent light was seen on the surface of Mars in 1894. For ten nights running there were jets of fire, actually missiles being fired at the earth, in the sky. People in Berkshire, Middlesex, and Surrey thought it a falling star when the first one landed. They were wrong. A great projectile, a Thing thirty yards in circumference, landed in the sandpits between Horsell and Ottershaw and Woking. It was hot and noises came from the inside. It had a dark and scaly incrustation. The wondering crowds who gathered to view the Thing saw one end begin to revolve slowly. It opened like a screw. First things like small gray snakes writhed out. Then, as the narrator of this Wells tale watched fascinated with the rest,

A big greyish, rounded bulk, the size, perhaps, of a bear, was rising slowly and painfully out of the cylinder. As it bulged up and caught the light, it glistened like wet leather.

Two large dark-colored eyes were regarding me steadfastly . . . it was rounded, and had, one might say, a face. There was a mouth under the eyes, the lipless brim of which quivered and panted, and dropped saliva. The whole creature heaved and pulsated convulsively. A lank tentacular appendage gripped the edge of the cylinder, another swayed in the air. . . . There was something fungoid in the oily brown skin, something in the clumsy deliberation of the tedious movements unspeakably nasty. Even at this first encounter, this first glimpse, I was overcome with disgust and dread.

People advanced to befriend the visitors, but the Martians—more advanced than earth people—loosed a heat ray on them. A group under a white flag was burned out of existence in a flash of fire that charred the earth. The artillery sent to attack the invaders was sent into flames by heat and invisible light. Incased in great stalking machines, walking tripods higher than houses, the Martians advanced spewing death and destruction. Whole towns and their inhabitants were obliterated as the tripods marched on London. There were scenes of horror on the choked roads as terror-stricken millions fought to abandon the largest city in the world.

Trapped under the ruins of a house with a curate and an artilleryman who had somehow escaped, the Narrator saw the Martians clearly. They were huge round heads about four feet in diameter, no nostrils, one big ear behind the head, sixteen whiplike tentacles, really their hands, about their mouths. Because they had no muscles to exert and bring on fatigue, the Martians had no need of sleep. They brought manlike creatures with them which they devoured for food.

The valiant artilleryman, a Wells puppet, says that the weak, the clerks, would give in. The Martians would probably treat them kindly and make pets of them. None of that for him. He and a few others would fight and survive. They would preserve the human breed. "We must make great safe places down deep, and get all the books we can, not novels and poetry swipes, but ideas, science books." Fortunately such extremes proved unnecessary. The Martians, who lived, of course, on a germ-free planet, succumbed to the bacteria to which human beings have become inured.

Today, at considerable expense and with the expenditure of considerable effort, rockets and men are being readied to fly to the moon. They are a little late. H. G. Wells was on the moon and deep inside it well over sixty years ago. In *The War of the Worlds* he had brought creatures from another planet to this one. He reversed the trip and in *The First Men in the Moon* sent two Englishmen into space. Dispensing with the fuss, bother, and taxpayer subsidization of rockets, he invented a substance opaque to gravitation. In a sphere built with this substance the scientist Cavor and the rather unscrupulous young businessman Bedford (the man of business is usually unscrupulous in Wells's tales) fly to the moon.

The mooncalfs they find on the surface are monstrous creatures of low intelligence. The large antlike Selenites, who live and work in caverns and tunnels of the interior, are the real rulers on the moon. As large as men, the Selenites, grotesque but highly intelligent, come in many forms, for the young are deliberately distorted into shapes best adapted for the work they are chosen to do.

The two men survive a series of adventures among these creatures and the strange plants on the moon and regain the surface. The innocent and well-meaning Cavor is injured, but Bedford manages to regain the sphere of "Cavorite" and somehow to pilot it through infinite space back to England.

Bedford's one thought is to return and fill the sphere with the limitless gold he and Cavor had found on the moon, but unexpected loss of the sphere and a series of strange messages delay his departure. Through a Dutch electrician whom he does not know, Bedford receives something much like radio messages transmitted from his erstwhile companion who had become the man in the moon.

Cavor had been captured by the Selenites. Two of

them, Phi-oo and Tsi-Puff, insects about five feet tall with large heads and short legs, had taken him in charge, quickly learned English, and brought him before the Grand Lunar. The messages cease when they are deliberately jammed by other radiations from the moon. It is quite possible that when astronauts land on the moon they will find Cavor still there, or at least be able to learn about his fate from descendants of Phi-oo and Tsi-puff.

Events are not as frightening as the life forms with which Wells peopled his fantasies. The Selenites, the Morlocks, and even the beautiful Eloi instill horror. Worst of all are the Beast Men, or perhaps the mad Moreau and the degenerate Montgomery. All of them are the imagined creatures of a student teacher of biology who, as he so often reminded his readers, had studied under T. H. Huxley.

Wells could not create character. The human beings in his science fiction are merely names. They have no distinct individualities. In these stories Wells seems not so much to lack sympathy with human life as to have no interest in it. His creatures of outer space or the distant future resemble men and women, but they are reptilian or beastly. Wells endows them with intelligence but with all of the worst and few of the better other human attributes. They are biological possibilities but without moral sense or aesthetic sensitiveness. Wells was not then or later deeply concerned with either.

There is a screen of generalities and there is the laboratory experiment attitude in Wells's science fiction. He throws a cloud of "science" over his ingenious tales but gives little actual explanation of the phenomena he presents. Evidently because he knew of none or there was none to give, he ignores supporting detail.

Except for *The Invisible Man*, these science-fiction stories are told in the first person, a device which Wells used generally in his fiction. It lends verisimilitude to narration. His story eases from the familiar, as told by an evidently trustworthy observer, to the fantastically unfamiliar. Often the narrator expresses skepticism but talks as if he must tell what he has actually and honestly experienced. His listeners may be somewhat skeptical at first too, but soon everybody, the storyteller, those who hear him, and the reader, is convinced. Thus credibility is established.

In a basic sense these science-fiction thrillers are out of Darwin and Huxley via the intelligent, ambitious, and materialistic H. G. Wells. They gave readers of the 1890s and the early 1900s something new, different, and exciting. They brought H. G. Wells the quick fame and the financial rewards that he was after.

4

Like a landowner inspecting his property, H. G. Wells traveled space, time, and the reaches of biological evolution with a kind of proprietary satisfaction. He did not come down to earth until he had exhausted their possibilities. When with equal aplomb he limited himself to this small world, he became almost simultaneously both a novelist and a Prophet. (Once more only an initial capital will suffice.)

Wells was so excited that when in 1896 he went abroad for the first time in his life he kept shaking hands with the friends who had come to see him and his wife off from Charing Cross station in London. In Rome they stayed with George Gissing, ill-fated romantic novelist and author of *The Private Papers of Henry Ryecroft*. The travelers saw France and Switzerland, then on their return moved from Woking to a roomy house in Worcester Park. For the first time Wells had a study of his own to work in, but he did not spend all his time in it.

Though he tried many times, Wells could not work by set routine. He worked intensely when he could. When

H. G. Wells and "Jane."

he could not, he played. Sometimes he did no writing for days on end. He walked. He cycled. He had had a tandem bicycle built, and he and his wife propelled it together. He grew ill not long after their return from Italy, and thinking to dispel his lassitude by exercise, he and Mrs. Wells started off on a cycling tour.

On the road Wells caught cold. The cyclists managed to get as far as Lewes, then Seaford, but there he had to give up. His side ached. His temperature mounted. As Dr. Collins had suspected that it might, the crushed kidney was acting up. Wells telegraphed Dr. Henry Hick, a physician friend of Gissing's, and cared for by his wife, managed to get to Hick's home in New Romney by train. At first Hick thought an operation was indicated, but the surgeon whom he brought up from London for consultation advised against it. Wells was put to bed in the Hicks' home. There, reading and sketching, writing as he could, he remained for six weeks.

One day his wife came downstairs and exclaimed that "H. G.," as she and his intimates called Wells, had read all he could. He was restless and bored. Was there anything about to keep him amused? In the playroom she and Mrs. Hick found a set of children's watercolors. Mrs. Wells exclaimed that they were just the thing. They would keep her husband busy for hours. She carted the watercolors upstairs.

A few days later she brought down and gave to the Hicks' small daughter, to whom it was dedicated, *The Adventures of Tommy*, written and illustrated by H. G. Wells. A delightful little child's book, the colored illustrations as bright and whimsical as the story is charming, it was not published until Marjory Hick was old enough to need money for her medical education. Then *The Adventures of Tommy* went through many editions as a popular children's book at Christmas. It was reissued in attractive format by a New York publisher in 1967.

Wells was ill and grateful. Gentle and affectionate, *Tommy* does not sound like the argumentative, indignant, and often pugnacious H. G. Wells who was on the way.

On the advice of Dr. Hick, Wells did not return to Worcester Park. In fact, he never entered what had been his home there again. Instead, the Wellses went by carriage to Sandgate, boarded for a time at this shore resort, then moved into a small furnished house called Beach Cottage. They moved into larger Arnold House, still in Sandgate.

Wells's health improved. He had survived what proved to be the last serious illness to beset his early career, and he was determined to have no more such nonsense. As he put it in his autobiography, he gave up dying there and then. Wells never died again as long as he lived.

He got back to the writing which had been interrupted by his misadventure. *Love and Mr. Lewisham* was the first of his serious, realistic, and contemporary novels as opposed to his science-fiction romances. It was also the first of his long line of autobiographical novels.

Mr. Lewisham taught in a grammar school which was actually the Midhurst Grammar School. He lived where Wells had lived over the sweet shop in West Street. Like Wells, Mr. Lewisham drew up a "schema" or schedule of activities and objectives. Like Wells he went to London as a science student, and Wells describes his hero in the laboratory of the Normal School of Science as he had known it.

As it had done with Wells, passionate love knocked Lewisham, his schema, and his ambitions into confusion. The contrast comes in at this point. Unlike Wells who abandoned his marriage when it proved unsatisfactory, Mr. Lewisham was trapped. There were children. He became immolated in a domesticity which effectively killed any attempts at a freer and fuller life. Wells was picturing something he had feared and escaped, and which he escaped each time it threatened to become a constraining reality.

When Arnold House failed to be all they wished, Wells decided to build. He had the money now, and he always had more than he needed of enthusiasm for a new venture. He selected a site between Folkestone and Sandgate and building operations were started. Daily Wells watched his house going up with deep satisfaction, sharp impatience, and mounting horror. Carpenters and masons worked just as they had worked for centuries. Building was not scientific and modernized. Wells grew eloquent about it, but warm satisfaction stilled his complaints. Proudly he took visitors to watch the progress being made on construction of his house. He had come a long way from Bromley.

Spade House, as Wells named it, was completed in 1900. It was a stucco house with a long sloping red roof. Inside, there were large, low-ceilinged rooms. Outside there was a large garden, a rock garden, a tennis lawn, and the sea. On clear days Wells could see the outline of the coast of France.

At Spade House, H. G. Wells swam, bicycled, talked, played charades, indulged his new hobby of photography, and wrote and wrote and wrote. Many of his most important books were written here. His son George Philip Wells was born in July 1901 and his second son, Frank Richard Wells, in November 1903.

Life was intense at Spade House and often uproarious. Guests came on the weekends to disport themselves with games and talk. Henley, Frank Harris, Shaw, Dorothy Richardson, Grant Allen, Gissing, and other writers and editors descended on Spade House for croquet, badminton, field hockey, what Wells called "barn ball," and all the other outdoor and indoor sports he played with strenuous abandon. Jovial, beginning to get fat, always untidy in baggy tweeds, talking breathlessly in his high-pitched voice, Wells seemed never to tire.

He seemed never to stop. Laughing, gesticulating, he talked endlessly, usually in long, excited monologues. Then with the excitement he had generated stimulating him as well as his friends, he would suddenly disappear. He'd had an idea and was back at his writing desk. He might reappear before he had been missed or he might be gone for some time before he returned with his arms full of bright costumes in which he demanded everyone dress up for dinner or an impromptu picnic. Even before they had finished dressing he might start another argument or discussion with the merriment and the protestations mounting as people tried to shout each other down or gave up to start yet another game. Before the new excitement was over he might disappear into his study again. Brilliantly alive now, Wells was supercharged and prolific.

There was one stable factor through all the weekend uproar and the alternate work and play on other days. In *The Book of Catherine Wells* he has described the part played by his wife during these years.

> She stuck to me so steadily that in the end I stuck to myself. I do not know what I should have been without her. She stabilised my life. She gave it a home and dignity. She preserved its continuity. Not without incessant watchfulness and toil. I have a hundred memories of an indefatigable typist carrying on her work in spite of a back-ache; of a grave, judicial proof-reader in a garden shelter, determined that no slovenliness should escape her.

Much of Wells's elation in these years sprang from his success. The well-known J. B. Pinker was his friend and literary agent. Frankly commercial despite his socialistic beliefs, Wells was writing for money and getting it. He gloated over the large sums he was being paid now for his writing and plotted to get more. A new opportunity offered, and he grabbed at it.

At the end of each calendar year or the beginning of the next, chambers of commerce, other civic bodies, governmental organizations, and academic associations indulge themselves in an annual orgy of forecasting. They decide what will happen economically, politically, socially, meteorologically, astrologically, and, for all anyone knows, ornithologically, during the ensuing year. News-papers and magazines, sometimes radio and television, report their prognostications with awe and wonder.

As undoubtedly they will in December 1999 and the early months of 2000, professional and amateur fore-casters went on an uninhibited binge as the nineteenth century ended and the twentieth began. You can do at least one hundred times more with a century than you can with a year, and they did. Caught up in the enthusiasm, H. G. Wells decided he would try his head and hand at it too.

When he came back from the moon and the future to turn his blue-eyed attention to this globe, Wells found himself fortified in the strong convictions he had held before he went off with the invisible man and the all too visible Martians. He believed in science, all science, every science, and in the application of the scientific method to all of life. He believed that evolution would continue. There had been progress in the past. Progress would con-tinue to progress. He believed that biological and social advance was inevitable.

Wells believed in socialism. Individual enterprise for the benefit of the individual was out; collective enterprise for the collective good was in. Nationalism was outmoded and meaningless. There would have to be a world state, one country for all the world, instead of hundreds of countries warring and competing.

Wells believed all this, and he said so and a lot more in *Anticipations of the Reaction of Mechanical and Scientific Progress Upon Human Life and Thought*. First serialized in the *Fortnightly Review*, published as a book in 1902, *Anticipations* (as it is mercifully called) is a key Wells document.

With *Anticipations* H. G. Wells leaped spotlighted to center stage as a world Prophet. Still the journalist exploiting popular taste for his individual purse, Wells was something more in this book. He was the convinced thinker of large views proclaiming forcefully what he thought and confidently what he foresaw. This was the first major statement of the thesis he would defend year after year in book after book. It was a declaration of his essential attitudes and proof of his perceptiveness. *Anticipations* established the renown as a seer from which Wells could never extricate himself, nor did he wish to. The Prophet gloried in it and practised his clairvoyance with brash confidence all the rest of his life. He had earned the right. Sometimes Wells was ridiculously wrong. More often he was frighteningly correct.

In *Anticipations* Wells prophesied the triumph of automotive transport. When he wrote, the automobile was only a few years old. It was undependable. It was a smoking menace to men, women, children, and horses. It was a target of ridicule. Wells foresaw the automobile's becoming the principal means of land travel over a network of roads comparable to what in the United States we now call superhighways.

Wells foresaw the dissolution of large cities. The automobile and the telephone would make it possible for people to live at a distance from their work yet remain within quick and easy communication. It would no longer be necessary to maintain congested centers of population either for living in or for the conduct of business. He saw people moving into the suburbs, then into the country both to work and to play.

Wells believed that fundamental changes in domestic life would take place during the twentieth century. People heated their homes with wood and coal when he was writing *Anticipations*. He said they would use electricity both for heating their homes and for cooking. Long before the electric range became fact Wells wrote,

> Today cooking, with its incidentals, is a very serious business; the coaling, the ashes, the horrible moments of heat, the hot black things to handle, the silly, vague recipes, the want of neat apparatus. One always imagines a cook working with a crimson face and bare, blackened arms. But with a neat little range, heated by electricity and provided with thermometers, with absolutely controllable temperatures and proper heat screens, cooking might easily be made a pleasant amusement for intelligent invalid ladies.

Wells had not puttered in a laboratory for nothing. He was for the workable, the efficient, for new and improved engineering applications of scientific developments. Far ahead of the actuality he foresaw smaller and more convenient homes. There would be no servants. Practical housekeeping would be performed by mechanical devices.

Wells delved farther into the home, this time into its human composition rather than its furnishings and external functioning. Here he provoked a storm of criticism that was part of the attention paid to his first book of prophecy.

He said he believed that during the twentieth century the institution of marriage would change. There would be "a considerable relaxation of the institution of permanent monogamous marriage." Every household would not be made up of a man, a woman, and possibly children living forever in a fixed economic and social unit. Easing of the marriage and divorce laws would make other kinds of marriages possible and permissible. Some marriages might be permanent, others temporary. Not tradition and approved Victorian morality but the wishes of the people concerned would decide. By 1950, he wrote, the unmarried mother would not be held up to censure.

Wells always argued for the impersonal scientific attitude toward individual and social problems. Yet he was usually intensely personal in his impersonal views. He reached large conclusions on the basis of his own experience and inclinations.

Some of H. G. Wells's other prophecies in *Anticipations* were more startling, and they were woefully accurate. In 1900 he proclaimed that the twentieth century would see total wars, with nations pitting all of the energy and skills of their populations against each other.

His prediction was nearly true in 1914–1918, almost completely true during World War II, when whole peoples were organized for war, some conscripted into military service, others into war-connected activities. Industry was mobilized for the production of war matériel; civilian as well as military personnel were bombed. Cities

—notably the London Wells knew so well—were subjected to almost unceasing aerial attack and many cities, German as well as English, were virtually demolished.

Wilbur and Orville Wright did not make their first successful airplane flight at Kitty Hawk until December 17, 1903. Yet in *Anticipations* Wells foresaw both the sky dogfights of World War I and the formation flying of World War II. At the beginning of this century when it seemed a possibility almost as remote as the moon flight he described in his science fiction, H. G. Wells insisted that to be victorious in modern warfare a nation would have to seize command of the air. In the 1930s, Brigadier General William Mitchell was court-martialed for claiming as much.

Wells said that multitudes of balloons would be used in twentieth-century warfare to act as eyes for the artillery. He was right and then wrong. Balloons were used extensively in World War I to target artillery fire and to some extent early in World War II, but were then discarded as too vulnerable.

He envisioned the tank, which after long argument and much persuasion, the British built and used toward the end of World War I. Wells, who called them "ironclad fighting machines," was right there. He also foresaw squads of cyclists going into battle. There he was wrong. Motorcycles, then jeeps, then helicopters came too fast.

All through *Anticipations* Wells talked of "a republic that must ultimately become a world state of capable, rational men."

Men had dreamed of a world state long before this, but

Wells did more than dream. He seized on the idea of a world state as something which could become a practical reality. From this time on he talked of and fought for it. The idea of one terrestrial, all-inclusive government became the ruling passion of his life. It was his sanitized and computerized Holy Grail.

Wells detested what he saw as the outworn, the obscure, the emotion-ridden. He worshiped the rational, the efficient, and the different if he thought it was intelligible or thought that it would work.

There was always a clinical bareness and an antiseptic and prophylactic quality about the Wells outlook. He had no loyalty to the past and no sympathy with human weakness. The fittest survived. He was, he was convinced, fit, capable, and rational, and he wanted a world of biologically and logically fit men and women much like H. G. Wells.

Wells believed that human life would be held more cheaply in the twentieth century, and he was not appalled. A strong advocate of birth control and of the sterilization of the incurably diseased, insane, or incompetent, he thought that insane criminals should be killed and the useless poisoned. "The men of the new republic will not be squeamish either in facing or inflicting death, because they will have a fuller sense of the possibilities of life than we possess."

Wells was correct, of course, in his prophecy that human life would be held of less consequence in the twentieth century. Wholesale slaughter in wars and killing on city streets have become commonplace. He was wrong in his belief that death would be more freely inflicted either as punishment or deterrent to unpleasant social behavior. The death penalty has gone out of fashion.

As he would many times again, Wells attacked both school and university education. He had gone to school and he had been a schoolteacher. He was convinced that most schoolteachers of his time were second-rate and ineffectual. He had not attended one of the universities, but he was equally convinced of their culpable uselessness. He pled for more practical schooling than that provided by "the ignorant and pretentious blunderers of today" and for improvement in the universities, which he called mere cram schools.

"Education" was always the Wells panacea. He might not be in favor of God, Country, or Motherhood, with which it is usually combined in a sort of holy quaternary, but he was in favor of Education. In 1900 he even called for continuing adult education. "The three years of university and a lifetime of garrulous stagnation which constitutes the mind's history of many a public school-master, for example, and most of the clergy to-day, will be impossible under the new needs."

Though Wells talked in terms of a world state in *Anticipations*, he often continued to think in terms of nations and to assume competition among them. He reflected much of the modern attitude toward education. He saw it not so much as development of the capacities of the individual but as a cure for social ills and a general strengthening of the competitive assets of a country. Some of what he says in this passage might have come from contemporary government propaganda or from the prospectus of an educational institution anxious to show its patriotic selflessness in soliciting students.

The nation that produces in the near future the largest proportional quota of educated and intelligent engineers and agriculturists, of doctors, schoolmasters, professional soldiers, and intellectually active people of all sorts ... that most readily picks over, educates, sterilizes, exports or poisons its people of the abyss ... that by wise interventions, death duties and the like, contrives to expropriate and extinguish incompetent rich families ... that turns the greatest proportion of its irresponsible adiposity into social muscle . . . will certainly be the ascendant or dominant nation before the year 2,000.

Wells was advocating education. He was also advocating socialism with a strong touch of totalitarianism.

Anticipations ends on an odd note. Wells had long since rejected traditional religion. For him there was no all-seeing God, no afterlife, no heaven, hell, reward or punishment. Either he was just trying to end his long book neatly or trying to avoid giving further offense to the many he had already offended. Perhaps, superstitiously, he was spilling a last-page oblation to the fates which would determine how much of his soothsaying was truth-saying. He may even have acknowledged a sort of over-ruling life force when he wrote piously, "The world has a purpose greater than happiness; our lives are to serve God's purposes."

Whatever he meant or whether he meant anything at

all, Wells had made the first bald statement of his convictions. He had laid down the guidelines of the thought he would pursue, and by omission, indicated all the departments of life he would neglect or of which he was unaware. Confidently and courageously the Prophet had spoken—and he had amply demonstrated both the reach of his intelligence and his often astounding prescience.

5

When H. G. Wells plotted his career as an intellectual, he did not have to set limits to it because of lack of talent in other directions. His interests were as diverse as his mind was active and his pen prolific. His abilities were equal to them all.

He was an avowed socialist. He was a social planner. In *Anticipations* he has showed himself something of a political scientist and a world prophet as well. He was considered to be a leading advocate of what was then called "free love." Depending upon their backgrounds, circumstances, and temperaments, readers applauded his moral liberalism or denounced his roseate immorality.

At Spade House, sizzling with energy, his Irish-blue eyes agog as he explained to his guests all in the world that needed changing and all that it behooved them to do about it, Wells talked shrilly, gesticulated wildly, and wrote as if a demon possessed him. He was good, he said, for about three books a year, and he was making his quota or more. He was hurrying to keep up with his success. Wells seemed not to realize for some time that success had to hurry to keep up with him. He had appeared as the English Jules Verne. He had appeared as the Prophet. He was already playing to packed houses in a new role.

Once I lent a book which delighted me and which I had read many times. It was never returned. I bought another copy of *The History of Mr. Polly*. When reading it again fired my enthusiasm anew, I lent it to someone who, I felt, should not live another day without knowing Mr. Polly. That second copy never came back either. This proves that it is unwise to lend a book you value. It also proves that *The History of Mr. Polly* by H. G. Wells is worth stealing.

In his science fiction Wells reported and enlarged upon the universe he had discovered in Midhurst and in the Normal School in Kensington. In *The History of Mr. Polly* Wells reported in fictional form on his own and his brothers' experiences in the drapery trade. In another sense, he reported also on his early reading of Charles Dickens, for here he is the humorist who, like Dickens, has some serious social purpose but at the same time appreciates the comedy of eccentric individuals in conflict or accord with life.

Mr. Polly did not come first among Wells's novels of the first decade of this century, but it is one of the most characteristic and perhaps the best of his non-didactic productions during those years.

Mr. Polly, of course, is H. G. Wells in one of his many roles. He is short and rotund, flippant, disgruntled, dissatisfied. Like Wells, he lacked efficient schooling and was very conscious of it. Like Wells he read. Like Wells he spoofed the pronunciation of words when he was unsure, making a gay game of his embarrassment. Mr. Polly endured a dismal apprenticeship. His marriage was unsatisfactory. The shop he finally came to own was a failure. Like Wells, Mr. Polly decided to change all that, and he did.

He burned his bridges behind him. It was not actually a bridge but the haberdashery shop in High Street, Eastbourne, which he had kept for fifteen years. He did not burn down his dull and wholly unsatisfactory wife Miriam—a cousin—but left her to collect the insurance on the shop and on a husband disappeared and presumed dead. The scenes in which Mr. Polly performs as a highly unskilled arsonist are wondrously funny. So are many of the scenes, given in a long flashback, of the hero's earlier years.

His crimes successful, Mr. Polly takes to the road. He has various adventures, but they are as nothing to those he enjoys when he comes finally to a haven at the Potwell Inn. On a river and a favorite haunt of picnickers and walkers, the Potwell is reminiscent of Surly Hall, the inn kept by Wells's Uncle Tom near Eton. There Wells had flirted with his girl cousins, read widely in an illustrated set of Dickens, and met the famed Ellen Terry when the actress was staying in the inn while she studied a part.

The plump woman who owned the Potwell needed a handy man, and balding little Mr. Polly needed a home. It was an ideal arrangement with a bad flaw in it. His employer's nephew was released from the reformatory and returned to claim his own.

Wells divided the contest for possession of the Potwell Inn into three campaigns. The first ended when, after a ludicrous fight at close quarters, Mr. Polly shoved Uncle Jim into the river with a broom. The second was the Battle of the Dead Eel. The third was the Night Surprise. Wells described each of these campaigns in glorious detail.

Uncle Jim's verbose bellicosity is matched only by Mr. Polly's abject terror and then his desperate courage. The pictures of Uncle Jim wallowing pitifully and profanely in the river and of Mr. Polly waddling around the inn at as high a speed as he can manage with bellowing Uncle Jim in pursuit are lovely. The Battle of the Dead Eel is the happiest thing in a happy book.

Uncle Jim appears in all his truculence grasping a dead eel by a piece of newspaper wrapped around its tail. Striking upward and hard he lays about him. When one indignant guest dares intervene, the eel "struck the spectacled gentleman under the jaw with a peculiar dead thud." A party of girls scream for "Horace!" but Horace too goes down.

> . . . a woman's heart was stirred, and a pink parasol drove hard and true at Uncle Jim's wiry neck, and at the same moment the young man in the blue shirt sought to collar him and lost his grip again.
>
> "Suffragettes," gasped Uncle Jim with the ferrule at his throat. "Everyone!" and aimed a second more successful blow at Mr. Polly.
>
> "Wup!" said Mr. Polly.

That monosyllable is one of the most expressive in all of H. G. Wells.

The righteous triumph. Uncle Jim is arrested for stealing a hatchet and sent back to jail. Mr. Polly is left secure with the fat woman in their Potwell paradise. As it must sometimes in order to preserve its rather tarnished reputation, poetic justice prevails.

Wells, who never forgot and never forgave his early draper days, used them to happy effect in another of his humorous novels. A companion novel to *Mr. Polly, Kipps* must be ranked next to it for rendering of semirealistic story and of caricature.

Arthur Kipps is brought up in New Romney (where Wells had been ill) by an aunt and uncle who keep a stationer's shop much like Atlas House in Bromley. He is sent to the pretentious but tenth-rate Cavendish Academy. His best friend is Sid Pornick, son of a nearby haberdasher. Kipps has some boy and girl passages with Sid's sister Ann before he is shipped off as apprentice in the Folkestone Drapery Bazaar.

Suddenly Kipps inherits a fortune from his maternal grandfather. The comedy—and the tragedy—is that Kipps is unprepared. He is uneducated. He talks dialect English. He tries to learn the ways of society by hiring a social climber named Coote to tutor him. He becomes engaged to the hitherto unapproachable Helen Walsingham.

Kipps manages to carry off some of the obligations of a man of wealth but fails completely to ape socially acceptable mores and manners. He meets Ann, now a housemaid, breaks his engagement, marries Ann. They are like wondering children as they move into a magnificent new home.

Ladies come properly to call on the new Mrs. Kipps and leave their calling cards. Caught unaware, Ann can not face the appalling ordeal of greeting them. In tears she tries to explain to her husband.

"And me all painty and no cap on and nothing, neither missis nor servant like. There, Artie, I could 'a sunk through the floor with shame, I really could. I could 'ardly get my voice. I couldn't think of nothing to say but just 'Not at 'ome,' and out of 'abit like I 'eld the tray. And they give me the cards and went, and 'ow I shall ever look that lady in the face I don't know. . . . And that's all about it, Artie! They looked me up and down, they did, and then I shut the door on 'em."

Kipps's disappointment grew. "You did ought to 'ave known better than that, Ann! You reely did."

Wells has Kipps and Ann say "fousand" for "thousand" and makes other concessions to their use of their native tongue. Usually the dialect Wells affects throughout the book is easy to translate, but he sometimes loses the reader. The uninitiated may read along for some time before they realize that "butted toce" is only "buttered toast."

Both of these endearing innocents know that they are " 'ardly suited," as Ann says, to the position in life they feel forced to assume. Happiness comes with the loss of most of Kipps's fortune, retreat to a setting they understand and enjoy, and new riches from an unexpected source.

In the fashion of Thackeray and Dickens, Wells comes out from behind the scenes sometimes in *Kipps* to lec-

ture directly to the reader. Society should give its drapers'
apprentices a decent education and a decent chance.
It should do the same for its housemaids. The run of respectable society people are usually stupid or villainous.
Even this does not spoil the book. *Kipps* is an amusing and
a touching tale. Perhaps because Wells is reminiscing
fondly of the kind of people among whom he grew up and
whom he knew thoroughly, *Kipps* has an especial sureness. *Kipps* and *Mr. Polly* have a humor that is characteristic of H. G. Wells in too few of his books, and a gentle-
ness that is not characteristic of H. G. Wells at all.

Wells need never have studied in Midhurst and London
or taught A. A. Milne in his father's school or worked for
Briggs in order to write these novels. He had been Kipps,
and he was always in many ways Mr. Polly. He had grown
up among people like these as one of them. He understood
them with his emotions as well as with his quick mind.

He needed more experience than he could have gained
in shop, laboratory, and classroom to write *Tono-Bungay*
in 1908, and some of his other later novels. He gained that
experience of the larger world and the kinds of very articulate people in an important part of it as a result of
Anticipations.

When Sidney and Beatrice Webb read *Anticipations*,
they were enthused. Here was a new writer, a new mind,
forcibly expressing the socialistic ideas that they held and
earnestly taught. The Webbs jumped on their bicycles
one Sunday morning and pedaled from London out into
the country to find H. G. Wells.

Born in London in 1859, educated in Germany and
Switzerland, Sidney Webb was a government employee, a

member of the London County Council, and a lecturer at London University. In 1892 he had married Beatrice Potter, a social worker a year older than he who had come from near Gloucester. Both were convinced socialists. Both were seriously intent on bettering the lot of the worker. Together they produced essays, tracts, and books on political economic, and social subjects. They served on governmental committees investigating working conditions. They helped found the London School of Economics and Political Science. They led, they almost *were*, the Fabian Society.

The intent of the Fabian Society, with its star performer George Bernard Shaw, was to socialize England by political means. The society was modern, thoughtful, intellectual. In the third century B.C. the Roman dictator Fabius had successfully avoided direct engagements with his enemy Hannibal. He had harassed his antagonist and employed successful defensive campaigns. The Fabians approved and used his tactics. They would make England a socialist state not through revolution or direct conflict but through evolution—progress in political thought and action.

Wells, who had been stimulated by Fabian thought in his student days, eagerly accepted the Webbs' invitation to become a member of the Fabian Society. With Shaw as one of his two sponsors, he joined enthusiastically. He and Shaw, who was ten years his senior, had been friends for years. Wells distrusted Shaw's annihilating wit and his platform flippancy, but basically their ideas were the same. Both were socialists. Both were talkers. They were

H. G. Wells at about age thirty.

impatient of tradition and the past. They were for mind over sentiment.

They were widely diverse in appearance and in temperament. Six feet one inch, Shaw seemed taller because he was so lean. He was red-headed and redbearded. A Dublin Anglo-Irishman, Shaw had come to London with his mother when he was twenty. First a newspaper music critic, then a drama critic, he had become a novelist, then a playwright. When Wells joined the Fabians, Shaw had already written *Candida*, *The Devil's Disciple*, *Arms and the Man*, *Caesar and Cleopatra*, *Captain Brassbound's Conversion*, and other of his famous plays with their long and provocative prefaces. One of his five novels, *Cashel Byron's Profession*, about a prizefighter, had become well known. His *Man and Superman*, in which woman rather than man is pictured as the pursuer, came out in 1903, and his *Pygmalion* would one day become the musical, *My Fair Lady*.

Shaw was electric. He was a brilliant speaker. He was to infuse a whole generation with his sharpness, his irreverence, his paradox, and his satire. Wells was to influence the same generation with his comparable attacks on accepted ideas and conventions, but there was a difference. A wit, Shaw appealed to the intellectual. Wells, only sometimes a humorist and always a serious teacher, affected mostly the newly educated, the undereducated, and those who got their first liberal education in social and world political ideas from Wells himself. The sophisticated Shaw amused himself and the world as he went along. Heavily serious about human progress and the world state, Wells was more determined than amused or amusing.

Besides her key participation in the Fabian Society, Beatrice Webb conducted a socialistic salon in London. She also organized the "Coefficients," a dinner club of writers and public men which had its first meeting in the London flat of Sir Edward Grey and Lord Haldane in Whitehall Court.

Wells was one of the twelve original members of the group which met monthly to dine and talk politics and socialism. With him in the Coefficients, which grew to have twenty-five members, were Sidney Webb, L. S. Amery, Bertrand Russell, Clinton Dawkins, Josiah Wedgwood, Lord Robert Cecil, Lord Milner, and others important in government, literature, finance, and science.

Wells mingled now with men of intellect and responsibility. Some were titled. A number held high governmental posts. Men of education and intellect, all of them aware of social change and some of them socialists or possessed of socialistic leanings, they were articulate and stimulating. At Fabian meetings, at the Webbs', at the Coefficients, Wells listened, absorbed, stored up knowledge of men and affairs. Nor did he take a back seat. A good Cockney, he was not intimidated by the awesome company he kept.

He also was now a man of accomplishment and reputation, and he paid deference to no one. He talked as much as any of them, probably more than some, and in the Fabian Society he quickly began to throw his weight—he had considerable now—around.

H. G. Wells was becoming a full man when, approaching forty, he came in 1906 to the United States for the first of many visits.

6

Wells came to the United States (like most Europeans he usually calls it America) in 1906 to write a series of articles for the London *Tribune*.

Like all travelers he saw what he saw and heard what he heard in terms of his own background, experiences, beliefs, and prejudices. With the disarming frankness which he shows in his autobiography, he says in *The Future in America*, "Remember always that I am an undiplomatic tourist of no special knowledge or authority, who came, moreover, to America with certain prepossessions."

Despite this accurate disclaimer, Wells was a perceptive observer and an accurate reporter. *The Future in America* was a sound book when he wrote it in 1906, and more than half a century later it is still a firm and reasonable appraisal of this country. It was not really about the future at all but about the United States as Wells saw it in what he called his search for realities. The title simply exploits his reputation as a prophet. Wells missed many of the realities in the United States, but those he found he put down fairly.

As James Russell Lowell noted long ago, visiting foreigners are usually condescending toward the United States. Beginning with Mrs. Frances Trollope, who was not condescending but contemptuous, English writers have felt themselves superior by right of birth. They are kept feeling that way by chronic self-delusion and assiduous practice.

Not without consciousness, perhaps, that he was a second Dickens boldly venturing toward the savage American shores, Wells read Dickens's *American Notes* as he crossed the Atlantic in the Cunard line's *Carmania*. He learned all about the stupidity and crassness of tobacco-chewing Americans, about the filth and corruption in American jails, and the absurdity of Congress, but he seems to have been little influenced by what he read. After all, Wells's father had once planned to emigrate to the United States and had gone as far as to build a chest in which to pack his belongings. The son might well have been born here, and in many ways Wells was rather American by temperament.

Including H. G. Wells, the *Carmania* carried 521 first- and second-class passengers, but 2,260 immigrants in steerage below decks. Like every beholder in those years, Wells was astounded by the number of immigrants pouring off the ships to be processed through Ellis Island in New York harbor, then herded into cities or scattered across the continent. Most were young and of hardy peasant stock. In one day 21,000 came; in one week, 50,000; in one year, 1,200,000. "They start digging and building and making. Just think of the dimensions of that!"

The unending supply of fresh population and the immensity of the country staggered Wells. He was impressed by New York with its skyscrapers, its rows of brownstone and marble houses, its magnificent clubs— but he had his doubts. "Noise and human hurry and a vastness of means and collective result, rather than any vastness of achievement, is the pervading quality of New York."

Boston annoyed him. He found its city planning pretentious, and he scorned Boston's love of the past. It was the present, but above all the future, that concerned him. Neither then nor later was he the friend of self-conscious culture, particularly literary and artistic culture. He got sick of hearing Longfellow quoted. In his opinion, Longfellow was not that good a poet. Wells discarded Boston, though it did give him one surprised realization.

> Come to think of it, Birmingham and Manchester are as new as Boston—newer; and London, south and east of the Thames, is, save for a little nucleus, more recent than Chicago—is in places, I am told, with its smoky disorder, its clattering ways, its brutality of industrial conflict, very like Chicago.

He looked at Chicago from the observation platform of the Pennsylvania Limited Express, but he did not visit the stockyards as certainly Dickens, with his penchant for visiting prisons, asylums, and sweatshops, would have done. Wells disliked seeing helpless animals slaughtered and said so. To the socialist, Chicago seemed less a distinct urban entity than one more example of the evils of capitalism and industrialism.

"Undisciplined"—that is the word for Chicago. It is the word for all the progress of the Victorian time, a scrambling, ill-mannered, undignified, unintelligent development of material resources. . . . All that is ugly in America, in Lancashire, in South and East London, in the Pas de Calais, is due to this, to the shoving unintelligent proceedings of underbred and morally obtuse men. Each man is for himself, each enterprise; there is no order, no prevision, no common and universal plan.

It was always a planned and ordered world that Wells wanted. Planned by whom and ordered to what end he could never quite say, but it had to be free of the evil of individuals working selfishly for their own gain in competition with other individuals working as selfishly to obtain the rewards they sought.

Wells saw accurately that in the United States there was neither peasantry nor aristocracy. The United States was all one big middle class with the rich on top and the poor at the bottom. Men strove to "make their pile," and like Carnegie or Rockefeller were admired for making it. The wealthy spent extravagantly, collected useless art—art was always useless to Wells—and made splendid but disordered philanthropic use of their ill-gotten gains by endowing foundations or leaving bequests to supposedly worthy causes. Wells found no excuse in this posthumous generosity for the original malfeasance of the money-makers.

Everywhere he went he saw graft, corruption, rudeness, and a dollar-driven society. He admitted that the mass of the American people were roughly prosperous and generally satisfied, but he was not satisfied, and everything which offended him he blamed on the "irresponsibility of the commercial kind."

Americans, he said, were unfailingly kind, but there was always a flash of hardness or harshness in them. They were callous as well as courteous. They were indifferent to brutality. They were intolerant of people different from themselves. They accepted dishonesty as in the nature of things. They ignored and slighted the Negro. As well he might, Wells attacked the vicious and irresponsible daily press of the time.

Wells had come to the United States equipped with journalist's credentials and many letters of introduction. He used them. He called on public men. He visited the universities. He inspected the comparatively new University of Chicago. He found Columbia University too busy. Universities anywhere seldom gained his approval, but he made an exception of Harvard, Harvard pleased him.

In Cambridge he talked with Harvard's President Charles Eliot but was disappointed that he could not see Professor William James, who was in California at the time. Next to T. H. Huxley, the pragmatic philosopher and pioneer psychologist was Wells's hero, and he said so often. In Harvard, Wells found many of the qualities which he had long accused the older English universities of lacking. Harvard, he said, was a living factor in the present and a force throughout the country. It had the constructive spirit and was conscious of playing a strong role in American life. Harvard opinion influenced public opinion through the press. H. G. Wells decided that he would let Harvard remain, and Harvard is still extant.

Dutifully, Wells went by car—unusual at the time but less difficult than traffic makes it today—from New York to inspect Washington Irving's Sleepy Hollow, about twenty-five miles up the east bank of the Hudson River. Sleepy Hollow bored him. He cared nothing for Ichabod Crane, Brom Bones, Rip Van Winkle, or Woolfert's Roost. He was not, he said, an antiquarian but a "go-ahead Englishman." For this reason, though he was pressed continually to go, he managed to avoid a visit to George Washington's home in Mount Vernon when he was in Washington.

Wells did all the sights in Washington. He found congenial society in the northwest section of the city. As Dickens had done when the city was little more than a mud slough, he watched Congress in session. He was no more admiring of that body than his literary predecessor had been. Congress was "no clearing house of thought at all," and Washington, to his mind, was intellectually dead. Its people "not alive to present and future things." He felt the United States should show more conscious effort toward the planned progress he thought it could achieve in a vast and only partly settled country.

Wells believed the United States would advance but not with the help of Washington. "The whole effect of Washington is a want of concentration, of something unprehensile and apart. It is on, not in, the American process."

Despite this unfavorable estimate, Wells liked President Theodore Roosevelt. Unimpressionable Cockney and rampant socialist though he was, Wells was often naive in his appraisal of world figures, up to and including Lenin, Stalin, and Franklin D. Roosevelt. He liked T. R. because he felt that the apostle of the strenuous life was honest and open to suggestion. "He sticks in my mind . . . as a very symbol of the creature will in man . . . In his undisciplined hastiness, his limitations, his prejudices, his unfairness, his frequent errors, just as much as in his force, his sustained courage, his integrity, his open intelligence, he stands for his people and his kind."

On the whole Wells liked the United States. If it would do as he wished and institute a planned economy and a planned society, he indicated that he might even approve the country. All it had to do was become a socialistic organization with its place in the world state and he would feel optimistic about its progress in human affairs. He did not feel that when he first saw it the United States had achieved perfection or even completion.

As he sailed down the Bay toward the mouth of the Narrows and Sandy Hook on his way back to England, Wells looked back at Manhattan.

And suddenly as I looked back at the skyscrapers of lower New York a queer fancy sprang into my head. They reminded me quite irresistibly of piled-up packing cases outside a warehouse.

7

Men have dreamed of perfection in the political state—of the ideal community—for a long time. Four centuries before the birth of Christ, Plato wrote his *Republic*. Because wisdom is the highest virtue, philosophers would rule in the ideal state. Below the philosophers would come the warriors, their virtue courage. The state would be a unit exacting discipline of all its members. Plato advocated the abolition of private property and the abolition of the family. All children would be brought up by the state. The state would give men and women the same education. Plato was no democrat. He considered democracy one of the poorest forms of government.

Sir Thomas More published his *Utopia* in 1516. More advocated communism, religious toleration, and like Plato, equal education for men and women. Early in the seventeenth century Sir Francis Bacon in *The New Atlantis* made science the key to the ideal state. William Morris plugged for socialism in *News From Nowhere* (1890) and Samuel Butler in *Erehwon* ("nowhere" backward) in 1872 pictured a land in which illness was considered a crime, crime treated as illness, and machinery had to be abolished before it seized control of man. In the classic American utopia, *Looking Backward* (1888), Edward Bellamy of Chicopee Falls, Massachusetts, pictured Boston in the year 2000. He postulated state capitalism and a state with no private enterprise, no crime, no disease, no poverty.

H. G. Wells knew all of these books. He was writing out of a long tradition and drawing ideas from Plato and the others when he wrote *A Modern Utopia*. He was also completing the outline he drew in *Anticipations*, further defining the conception of his world state.

In form *A Modern Utopia* is an odd book. The story of escape into a world of the future much resembling our own is narrated by "the Voice," and there is little confusion as to whom the voice belongs. At the beginning of the book its author is described as

> . . . a whitish plump man, a little under the middle size and age, with such blue eyes as many Irishmen have, and agile in his movements and with a slight tonsorial baldness—a penny might cover it—of the crown . . . for the greater part he bears himself as valiantly as a sparrow . . . his voice . . . is an unattractive tenor that becomes at times aggressive . . . hands that are just a little fat at the wrists.

Seldom unconscious of himself, Wells felt that in *A Modern Utopia* he was writing an important book. He said he intended it to have "a sort of lucid vagueness." Where story and setting are concerned, the book is more vague than lucid, but it is clear enough where Wells's socialistic ideas are laid down.

In Utopia the Voice and his companion the botanist, an ordinary, earth-bound individual, enter a world state on a separate planet. It is scientifically organized. All property is collectively owned. There are world authorities for housing, policing, and transportation. There are no politics, hence no politicians.

Utopia is not classless. There are four social classes: the creator class at the top, then the kinetic or engineering class, then the dull, and then the base. In other words, there are the inventive and creative, the doers, ordinary people, and the hopelessly incapable.

Education is universal. Everyone except an unteachable lowest three percent goes to college free. After education to about age twenty, everyone travels. People marry, but childless marriages are ended. There is almost complete sexual liberty. There are no dogs or horses. The air is clean and sparkling. Wells made everything in his utopia the opposite of all that he saw as ugly or unhealthy in London.

Most of *A Modern Utopia* is a series of essays on race, women, freedom, and the ordered efficiency of life on this other and better planet. Wells is particularly admiring of the Samurai—named for the warrior nobility of Japan—whom he presents as the rulers of his world state. As he describes them, these Samurai are a voluntary nobility. Unselfish and dedicated men enter this disciplined order of their own free will after they are twenty-five years of age.

The Samurai do not smoke, drink, or use narcotics. They continue with their education until they are twenty-four or twenty-five but must accept state responsibilities in their early twenties. They dress with simple distinctness. They remain young, healthy, and erect. Noble by competence and the will to serve, not by birth, they live by the "Book of the Samurai." They follow the rule of the things that must be done and the things that must not be done. They worship a mystical God. In the Book of the Samurai, Wells places the "Invictus" of his editor and friend, William Ernest Henley. Evidently, Wells, who had no taste in poetry, was stirred by its brave sentiment.

> Out of the night that covers me,
>   Black as the pit from pole to pole,
> I thank whatever Gods may be
>   For my unconquerable soul . . .

Wells saw in the large. Nothing was too big for H. G. Wells; most things were far too small. He wrote of the huge, the vast. As he said himself, he thought in outlines. He seldom attempted to fill them in. His was the grandiose concept, particulars he left to other and smaller minds. His imagination rampant, his basic ideas fixed early and un-alterably, Wells lost interest when it came to details. There is ambitious sweep in his thinking. There is seldom fineness.

Without explanation, the Voice and the botanist find themselves back in contemporary London. They come to in noisy and smoky Trafalgar Square. H. G. Wells, who had been in both Utopia on another planet and the United States in the western hemisphere, burst back into strenuous activity.

He returned to the jaunts and jollities of Spade House and to the unremitting exercise of his swift pen. Words streamed across the paper as he alternated between being prophet and novelist or compromised by being both at once. Things needed changing, and he intended to change them. In 1917, in a preface to Frank Swinnerton's novel *Nocturne*, he said, "Personally I have no use at all for life as it is, except as raw material. It bores me to look at things unless there is also the idea of doing something with them."

What Wells wanted to do something about now was the Fabian Society.

As he saw it, the Fabians talked too much and did too little. There was what he condemned as an intellectual dilettantism about the society. It thought too small. The Fabians thought in terms of bettering the lot of the working class. They talked admiringly and sympathetically of labor. They thought in terms of party politics. Though he later tried unsuccessfully for Parliament, Wells had no faith in the machinations of political parties. He wanted the Fabian Society to think in larger and more practical terms. He wanted it to be usefully effective.

All of the Fabians were socialists with a detestation of the profit motive and a religious belief in the collectivist state, but their attitudes toward socialism and the ways by which they wanted to attain it differed. If Wells thought the Webbs and Shaw were dilettantish, they thought him impatient and undisciplined. Shaw was truly a Fabian. He could wait and amuse himself and the world while he waited. Wells did not want socialism to evolve gradually and the world state to come some time in the distant future. He wanted them now.

The Webbs, with Shaw, wanted to permeate the political structure with their ideas, thus bringing about socialism through a political movement within the established framework. That was too tame for Wells. He wanted hard and fast action. He was not interested in converting politicians inside the system he considered absurd. His idea was to convert the people through slam-bang publicity and propaganda—much as he was trying to do in his books.

As a member of the executive committee of the society, Wells read a paper before it titled "Faults with the Fabians." Like most people, the Fabians were not enthusiastic about having their faults pointed out, especially by a comparative newcomer whose manners and morals some of them did not applaud. What began as a difference of opinion about the policies and practices of the Fabian Society became a factional and personal dispute. Wells and his followers were engaged in a power struggle with the Webbs and Shaw.

Wells demanded that the Fabians set up offices, hire a clerical staff, campaign for members, and disseminate socialistic propaganda. As vehemently, and perhaps a little jealously, he demanded that they stop imitating George Bernard Shaw. He attacked tiny, large-headed, humorless Sidney Webb, who with his dominant wife and Shaw had so long controlled Fabianism.

It was a battle for control. The Webbs and Shaw won. This was undoubtedly fortunate for the Fabian Society. By his own admission, H. G. Wells was incapable of working with other people. An individual who lived by expressing his individuality—something he would never have permitted in his world state—Wells would probably have proved from impractical to impossible in trying to direct a politically oriented organization, or for that matter, an organization of any kind.

Defeated, Wells resigned from the Fabian Society in September 1908. Shaw went on to become the playwright darling of the intellectuals; Sidney Webb was to enter Parliament, become Lord Passfield, and serve as secretary of state for the British dominions and colonies. Together, after a long stay there, the Webbs wrote a two-volume analysis approving communism in the U.S.S.R.

H. G. Wells went back to doing with redoubled force what he did best, which was being H. G. Wells.

8

With all this varied experience of people and places and the larger world of talk and ideas, all of it fresh and exciting, Wells could write his big novel now. From the first he planned a full-length story on the Thackeray-Dickens model, but all of it is H. G. Wells. *Tono-Bungay* is Wells's one major novel, and it is a major English novel of the early twentieth century.

Wells poured it all into *Tono-Bungay:* his Up Park background, the chemist's shop in Midhurst, the London science classes, his early marriage and its failure, the kind of people he had known when he was young together with the more complex individuals he had come to know in London, and what he had seen and heard of business and industry in England and in the United States. He added his socialism, adopted the first-person narrative he had used successfully in his science fiction, and produced a novel of sweep and force. *Tono-Bungay* is at once compelling story and indictment of unrestrained and unethical private enterprise.

George Ponderevo, who tells the story of Tono-

Bungay, escapes from menial servitude as a baker's apprentice, reappears at "Bladesover" just as H. G. Wells reappeared at Up Park after escaping the drapers in Southsea, and is apprenticed to his chemist uncle Teddy Ponderevo in "Wimblehurst," which is Midhurst. He passes examinations, studies science in London, even fails those studies in the end because of his love affair with the commonplace Marion.

Meanwhile his energetic, sizzling, fat little uncle has found the recipe for a tonic in an old book, added a kidney stimulant, and invented Tono-Bungay. Teddy Ponderevo bubbles to bursting with ideas for promoting and selling this marvelous concoction. He is absurd, likeable, a sort of innocent criminal. George Ponderevo, who is not innocent at all but a modern scientific man, joins his uncle in marketing what he knows is a worthless product.

The success of Tono-Bungay is wondrous. The schemers take over England a section at a time. They invade Scotland with "Tono-Bungay: Thistle Brand," which contains eleven percent pure alcohol. They conquer Ireland.

"You can GO for twenty-four hours a day on Tono-Bungay."

"Like Mountain Air in the Veins"

"Health, Beauty, Strength"

"Many people who are MODERATELY WELL think they are QUITE WELL"

The advertisements warned against druggists who sold advertised patent medicines which did more harm than good. What people needed was simply Tono-Bungay.

"We sold our stuff and got the money, and spent the money honestly in lies and clamor to sell more stuff," says George Ponderevo. Weakening the formula as they sold in greater and greater volume, they diversified. Soon there were Tono-Bungay Lozenges, Tono-Bungay Hair Stimulant, Tono-Bungay Chocolate, Tono-Bungay Mouthwash. They took Britain by storm, and the money poured in. Always looking for new products he could market, Teddy Ponderevo dumped his swelling capital into soaps, lotions, and shoe blacking.

George Ponderevo's school friend, the sculptor Ewart, tries cynically to help.

"There's all these patent grain foods,—what Americans call cereals. I believe I'm right, sir, in saying they're sawdust."

"No," said my uncle, removing his cigar, "as far as I can find out it's really grain,—spoilt grain. . . . I've been going into that."

The older Ponderevo goes finally into almost everything. Overflowing with imagination and self-confidence, cutting the corners of his conscience, he rises from glory to glory until he is a touted and courted public figure with vast sums invested in vast enterprises. Wells makes him the prototype of the big businessman. He is not a villain. He is a misguided fool. He rises to riches and power through the gullibility of the public and the culpability of the state which does nothing to control the actions of predatory capitalists. Teddy Ponderevo is rewarded by society for perpetrating giant swindles.

When his nephew suggests as much, he is hurt. "I'd like to know what sort of trading isn't a swindle in its way."

Ponderevo builds an enormous country house. With some of his petty cash he publishes a literary journal. He is besieged by adventurers seeking financial backing for dubious schemes. His nephew partially withdraws from the business to take up gliding, build a flying machine, and have an affair with a woman of the world he had first known while she was an unattainable upper-class girl and he a servant's son.

In *Tono-Bungay* Wells indicts the whole of business through condemnation of a disreputable enterprise which mushrooms into an uncertain financial empire ruled by a silly emperor. Through the character of George Ponderevo he glorifies the man of scientific interests and engineering achievements. In Susan, wife of the entrepreneur and aunt of the narrator, he creates one of the most amusing and sympathetic of all his characters. Susan Ponderevo is witty, whimsical, tender, understanding of both her nephew and her childlike husband. *Tono-Bungay* is a humorous novel. It is a serious novel. It is a sociological novel. It is a full and exciting novel of fantastic success, spectacular failure, balloons, speedboats, love affairs. *Tono-Bungay* is a caricature of the industrial age, a portrait of what Wells considered the intelligent modern man, and a comedy of comic characters in comic play.

The novel ends morally in vivid melodrama and flaming disaster. A strong story, it leaves a strong impression. An all-inclusive novel of large dimensions, *Tono-Bungay* has sweep and vigor beyond anything Wells had shown or would show again.

Like all of Wells's work, it is coarse in grain. Wells does not write through an episode but skirts it with bold disregard for substantiating detail. His narrator—it is one of the advantages of the first-person device—says often that he does not remember the small but only the large and significant. As usual with Wells, the writing itself is journalistic and arresting, not worked and polished. In his novels as in his life, H. G. Wells moved with a rush. Dash, crash, splash, and get on with it was his way. There are no subtleties or fine distinctions. In *Tono-Bungay* this treatment works. All the elements fuse. *Tono-Bungay* is a stalwart, forceful serio-comic story—and an impassioned socialistic tract.

As ebullient as Teddy Ponderevo at the top of his form and as charged with electric energy as any six men, H. G. Wells had hardly yet begun to fight. Though he liked his home in Sandgate and he and his family had been happy there, he feared stagnation and the dulling effect of habit in any environment, however pleasant. His greatly improved health no longer necessitated his living in the country or at the shore. In 1909, the year when *Tono-Bungay* was published, Wells sold Spade House and moved into London's Hampstead. After brief residence in temporary quarters, the Wellses took up residence in an eighteenth-century home in Essex, Easton Glebe.

In his early forties now and vociferously alive, Wells had so much to say he could hardly write it all down fast enough, but he got more of it said this same year in *Ann*

Spade House

Veronica, A Modern Love Story. This novel drew all of the attention, much of it scandalized, that Wells could have wished.

Women were important to H. G. Wells, both actually and as idea. His sympathy was all with what was then called "the new woman," woman emerging early in this century from the kitchen and nursery into the outside world of men and affairs. Wells not only helped the new woman on her way, but also helped create her.

Ann Veronica Stanley, daughter of a respectable solicitor in the London suburb of Morningside Park, was attractive, intelligent, willful, and rebellious. A science student at Tredgold Women's College, she commutes daily to classes. This does not suffice. Determined to live her own life, she leaves father and doting aunt after a domestic spat and goes into grimy lodging in London to live on her own.

In the eyes of the righteous this was scandalous conduct for a well-brought-up young lady in 1909. Ann does far worse. She becomes involved with a gentlemanly rake who lends her money then tries to collect the debt he feels she owes. She goes to jail as a suffragette rioting for votes for women. As a convenience she becomes engaged to a chivalrous older man. All this makes for a promising— or reprehensible—beginning which Ann follows bravely or brazenly to the end.

Admittedly Wells drew Ann and her predicament from life. Ann declares her love for her young instructor in biology who has already shown his ability to write. Separated from his wife after being named corespondent in a divorce suit, he is unable to obtain a divorce himself. Like Shaw, Wells saw woman as the pursuer, not the pursued. Ann pursues and the instructor, Capes, demurs but then capitulates. They elope for a honeymoon in the Alps. When they return to London, Capes quickly achieves literary and monetary success as a playwright. Everything comes out beautifully in the end.

It all seems pink-pretty now. The passionate love affair is as wooden and stilted as most love affairs in Wells's stories. Ann Veronica's daring seems naive and unenterprising. Capes is only another picture of H. G. Wells. It seemed far different to readers of *Ann Veronica* at the time.

The Victorians had idealized women, and the Edwardians still clung publicly to this attitude. Women, especially desirable young girls, were soft, dainty, and helpless. They were supposed to be passive and resigned. They were not expected to be direct and sexually aggressive. *Ann Veronica* was condemned in the press and from the pulpit. H. G. Wells and his heroine were vilified as immoral, dangerous, and disgusting.

Wells did not think they were. He thought they were clean and brave. He thought they were beautiful. He thought they were modern. Angrily he fought back. He accused his accusers. They accused him anew. The public furor did not hurt the sales of *Ann Veronica*. Entranced readers even went back and bought copies of his science fiction in the hope of discovering more racy adventures. *Ann Veronica* became a *cause célèbre*. In the public mind H. G. Wells came to stand for illicit sexual relationships, for "free love." There was a whispering campaign as well as a press attack against him. In some places and by some people Wells was socially ostracized.

Certainly, Wells was against conventional moral restrictions. He had made that clear in *Anticipations* and in *A Modern Utopia*. The difference was that in those books he had been speculating about the future. In *Ann Veronica* he had been reporting contemporary life and writing, presumably, from fact.

Wells emphasized his position—and paid off a few old scores—in his next significant novel.

9

Published as a book in 1911 after being serialized in the *English Review*, *The New Machiavelli* was a political novel and the first of Wells's major discursive novels. *Kipps* and *Mr. Polly* were recognizable humorous narratives. *Tono-Bungay* had the standard novel form of beginning, middle, and end with adventure, suspense, almost a plot. *The New Machiavelli* is narrative with story enough to make it a work of fiction but with discussion and argument the substance of the book.

Ideas overweigh incidents. The novel deals with contemporary events, incidents, and public figures. As he stays close to the material of his own life in fiction, Wells stays close to the headlined news and subjects of consuming interest at the time in his discursive novels. They are journalistic in approach and in treatment. This is one reason why some of his novels which had a powerful thrust at the time of their publication seem badly dated now. *Kipps*, *Mr. Polly*, and the essential story of *Tono-Bungay* are dateless because of their warmth and humor and the interaction of characters and incidents. *Ann*

Veronica and *The New Machiavelli* lack this essential substance.

A rumor that no publisher would accept *The New Machiavelli* after its serialization led to a large advance sale for the book. The public hoped for more scandalous revelations. Instead, they got a long essay on sex and politics with just enough narrative to hold the discussions together. *The New Machiavelli* is a bald and stark ("stark" was a favorite word with Wells) exposition of the author's position on social and political problems and his insistently repeated cures for them.

This time the narrator-hero is not a scientist-engineer but a politician of national standing. Born in "Bromstead," as Wells was born in Bromley, Richard Remington loses his father, as Wells nearly lost his, when the father falls from a ladder while pruning a grapevine when his wife and son are at church.

Remington goes to a school which sounds much like Henley House, in which Wells taught under J. V. Milne. While there he starts a school paper which a sixth former then takes over and makes successful by plagiarizing every other successful magazine. This opportunist is "Cossington" in Wells's novel. Obviously he is Alfred Harmsworth, who became Lord Northcliffe. Throughout *The New Machiavelli* Wells refers to prominent people by name or by transparent pseudonyms. "Evesham" is Arthur James Balfour, Conservative Prime Minister, later Foreign Secretary and First Lord of the Admiralty. Calling the aristocratic Evesham the most powerful political figure in England, Wells uses the character to express many of his own political ideas. The Coefficients appear in *The New Machiavelli* as the "Pentagram Circle."

After Cambridge, Remington, who is very bright, marries wealthy Margaret Seddon. Her money and connections make it possible for him to be elected a Liberal member of Parliament. Remington had met his wife first through his uncle's family, then five years later at the London socialist salon conducted by Altiora and Oscar Bailey.

Oscar Bailey is a political journalist who is in the civil service. His wife, Altiora, is handsome, sexless, and scheming. Wells's readers recognized the Baileys immediately as Beatrice and Sidney Webb.

Remington describes them acutely.

> Temperamentally the Baileys were specialized, concentrated, accurate . . . the Baileys, it seemed to me, loved a world as flat and metallic as Sidney Cooper's cows. If they had the universe in hand I know they would take down all the trees and put up stamped tin green shades and sunlight accumulators. Altiora thought trees hopelessly irregular and sea cliffs a great mistake . . .

Like Wells and like most of his heroes, Remington is quickly successful. In politics he is recognized as a coming man. He mingles on equal terms with the near great, the great, and the very great. Then to his loyal wife's consternation he deserts liberalism for what in his novel Wells calls "New Toryism." He moved over because he felt that through "constructive aristocracy" he could accomplish more quickly and surely what he wanted. What he wanted, of course, was the ideal, organized, and practically managed world state. Through Remington, Wells says:

> The old liberal definition of liberty was a trifle uncritical. Privilege and legal restrictions are not the only enemies of liberty. An uneducated, underbred, and underfed propertyless man is a man who has lost the possibility of liberty. There's no liberty worth a rap for him. A man who is swimming hopelessly for his life wants nothing but the liberty to get out of the water; he'll give every other liberty for it—until he gets out.

Long before this, H. G. Wells had taken Darwinism out of the merely biological into the social sphere. To this he had added an unshakable belief—imbibed almost unconsciously from the air around him—in the inevitability of human progress. A few years later he would interpret all human history as proof of this. Speaking in his own character as author he says in *The New Machiavelli*, "All the history of mankind, all the history of life, has been and will be the story of something struggling out of the indiscriminated abyss, struggling to exist and prevail over and comprehend individual lives—an effort of insidious attention, an idea of invincible appeal."

Personal rather than political conflict comes into the story when Isabel comes on the scene. A bright young girl who had worked zealously in his campaign for Parliament, she joins Remington in London after graduating with honors from Oxford. He gives her a job on the staff of the political magazine he has founded, and the usual Wellsian triangle results. Though she is hurt, Remington's wife proves as understanding as Wells thought women should be in such situations, but London is not as permissive when Remington's liaison with Isabel becomes known.

The Baileys are now Remington's personal as well as his political enemies. Altiora is pictured as vixenish and gossip-mongering about the affair. Other delighted friends spread the growing rumors assiduously. Wells is obviously and bitterly autobiographical here.

> I think there can be nothing else in life quite like the unnerving realization that rumour and scandal are afoot about one. Abruptly one's confidence in the solidity of the universe disappears. One walks silenced through a world that one feels to be full of inaudible accusations. One cannot challenge the assault, get it out into the open, separate truth and falsehood. It slinks from you, turns aside its face. Old acquaintances suddenly evaded me, made extraordinary excuses; men who had presumed on the verge of my world and pestered me with an intrusive enterprise, now took the bold step of flat repudiation. I became doubtful about the return of a nod, retracted all those tentacles of easy civility that I had hitherto spread to the world.

Remington's worried intimates try to talk him out of his romantic attachment. Britten, his old friend and his associate on the magazine, tries his best, but the passion is too strong. Remington is indignant as well as trapped. It is not he and Isabel but the lack of sex education and education in what he considers true morality that are at fault. It is social stupidity that prevents his keeping both Isabel and his gratifying political power and glory.

"This is a dirty world, Britten, simply because it is a muddled world, and the thing you call morality is dirtier now than the thing you call immorality." Remington makes his choice, and he and Isabel flee England.

Though it enhanced his reputation, added to his fortune, and widened his reading public, *The New Machiavelli* did nothing to endear H. G. Wells to his critics. There was renewed outcry against him. He was attacked in the newspapers and from the pulpit for a new display of eroticism. He was also attacked for his malice in the portrayal of living politicians and of people who had been his friends. Dislike for Wells personally mounted in some quarters, and Wells did not like it. Possibly it was to escape some of the unfriendliness manifested toward him and to live for a time in a more comfortable atmosphere that the Wellses spent the summer of 1911 in northern France.

10

By this time and through the 1920s into the 1930s four men dominated the English literary world. They were the popular writers whose books were read eagerly as they appeared, both in Great Britain and in the United States. They were public figures whose activities and comments were reported continually in the press. When they visited this country, as all of them did, they were front-page news, and their speeches and comments were headlined.

The four were George Bernard Shaw, John Galsworthy, Arnold Bennett, and H. G. Wells.

People went regularly to the theater, but Shaw's brilliant plays were more read than seen. Cleverness, glitter, paradox, sharp comment—these were Shaw. Galsworthy, quiet spoken, almost reserved, was a popular playwright but was best known for his *Forsyte Saga*, a novel trilogy, and *A Modern Comedy*, another trilogy. Educated at Harrow and Oxford, he was the aristocrat of the four. He was the historian of the English upper-middle class to which he belonged. Shy and handsome, he modeled his writing on the Russian novelists, particularly Turgenev.

Sensitiveness and compassion informed his work. Most readers knew Soames Forsyte and other members of the Forsyte family.

Arnold Bennett, Wells's lifelong friend, was a different matter. Son of a solicitor, Bennett was born in the English industrial Midlands. Married to a French wife, living mostly in France, Bennett wrote after Balzac and other French realists but wrote about the English pottery towns in which he had grown up. His two best novels, and they are fine novels indeed, warm, full, substantial, and convincing, are *The Old Wives Tale* and *Clayhanger*. Others —*These Twain, Hilda Lessways, Riceyman Steps*—are almost as good as his best.

No less popular, no less influential than the others, H. G. Wells was by far the least of the four as a writer.

Wells wrote too fast, too hard, and too journalistically. His greatest lack as a novelist was his inability to create character. As he admitted in his autobiography, "Exhaustive character study is an adult occupation, a philosophical occupation." Wells was incapable of it because he did not understand character, had not the ability to create character, and had no interest in it. He had no interest in art for art's sake or even in art for the sake of better writing. He was too intent on selling his wares. He was the teacher and preacher who necessarily used books to attain the financial success he valued as much and pursued as hotly as anyone else, and to give him the position of authority he needed to obtain a hearing for his convictions.

Yet Wells wished to be considered an important novelist as well as a prophet, sociologist, and political scientist.

As he said, he could never feel honestly inferior to anyone. He did not feel inferior to Bennett, with whom he corresponded at length about their writing. Though he succeeded Galsworthy as president of the international P.E.N. club of writers, he seems hardly to have known him. He could never have approved a university-educated gentleman who wrote in gentlemanly fashion of the kind of gentlefolk Wells detested. Wells certainly did not consider himself inferior to the mercurial Shaw against whom he had pitted himself in the Fabian Society.

Arbiter of literary taste at the time and foremost exponent of the novel as a work of art was Henry James. Born to wealth in New York, he was the son of Henry James, Sr., eccentric and philosophic essayist, and the brother of William James of Harvard, whom H. G. Wells so admired. An expatriate who took up permanent residence in Europe in 1875, Henry James is usually considered the foremost American novelist and critic of the novel. His was the international theme, and he wrote usually of the "jet set" of Victorian and Edwardian times, describing the rich and cultured society he knew best.

James's interest was seldom in story but in character, and he developed his novels as paintings, extracting the meanings, and all the subtleties and shadows of meaning, out of the social situation in which he involved his rarefied characters.

Author of many novels, James was already eminent when Wells was still a young dramatic critic. He was fifty-five years old, Wells thirty-two when they met. They became intimates when Wells moved to the country not far from Rye where in his exquisitely appointed Lamb House, James lived the life of an English gentleman. Impressed by Wells's writing, particularly by *A Modern Utopia*, James welcomed Wells as a younger craftsman and encouraged him.

Wells liked being accepted at Lamb House along with Gissing, Stephen Crane, Joseph Conrad, and other young writers, but he understood little of what James attempted in his writing. Much of it transcended the range of his interests or his abilities. There were other differences. James was well-bred, highly educated, and wealthy. He was considerate and gently courteous. He was sometimes pontifical, and like most people, often absurd in his own way. Wells was of ruder, cruder, and, he felt, stronger stuff. James was tentative and deprecatory. Wells pushed and pushed hard.

The older writer read and appraised Wells's books as they appeared and talked to him or wrote to him about them. He admired their good qualities, but he was sometimes shocked at their disorderliness. There was little art in them. They showed no unity of composition. Proud of his mounting success, Wells resented any but the most favorable criticism.

Henry James was particularly generous in his comments on *The New Machiavelli*. He wrote Wells:

> I have read you, I need scarcely tell you, with an intensified sense of that life and force and temperament, that fullness of endowment and easy impudence of genius, which makes you extraordinary . . . Your big

feeling for life, your capacity for chewing up the thickness of the world in such enormous mouthfuls, while you fairly slobber, so to speak, with the multitudinous taste—this constitutes for me a rare and wonderful and admirable exhibition.

The pugnacious Wells should have purred at the compliment from an acknowledged master craftsman of their trade. Instead, he became incensed when James went on to decry his use of the autobiographical form in the novel. He objected particularly to "autobiography brought, as the horrible phrase is, up to date." He asked more richness, more fullness, more imagination, more interpretation in a novel.

Wells defended himself in conversation at the Reform Club, where James usually stayed when in London, and he defended his loose, argumentative, and disputative fiction in "The Contemporary Novel," an article in the *Fortnightly Review* for November 1911. He had no use for the unified novel, whatever that was. He had practical use for the discursive novel. He did not say so in the article, but it was an effective weapon for a journalist and propagandist.

Wells knew nothing of art, which is all right. That he was proud of his ignorance is hardly as admirable—though that is part of what made him H. G. Wells. Another part was his easily wounded vanity.

James published an article on the younger writers in *The Times Literary Supplement* early in 1914. He was discussing a literary point, not indulging personal animus, when he said that both Arnold Bennett and H. G. Wells wrote formless, widespreading novels.

Wells took time out for a quick visit to Russia, which was not then a feared and darkly forbidding country suspected by and suspicious of the rest of the world. Wells liked St. Petersburg and Moscow. He was pleased with the towers and cupolas of the Kremlin. He liked the Russian people and the little black and gold shops. He liked almost everything he saw in Tsarist Russia and on his return persuaded F. W. Sanderson, headmaster of the Oundle School in which he enrolled his sons, to institute the teaching of Russian. He also let go completely at Henry James.

Wells published a book with a title almost as long as its varied content. Its full title, with only the first part italicized was: *Boon, the Mind of the Race, The Wild Asses of the Devil and the last Trump,* Being a First Selection from the Literary Remains of George Boon, Appropriate to the Times, prepared for publication by Reginald Bliss, with an Ambiguous Introduction by H. G. Wells. Into this miscellany Wells inserted a chapter called "Of Art of Literature, of Mr. Henry James."

In it he lampooned Henry James. Flailing about, he paid no attention to whether he hit above or below the belt. He ridiculed James, his writing, the characters in his novels, even his beloved Lamb House. He dispatched James's novels and his now almost classical criticism. James wrote only of the idle rich. They had no opinions on religion or politics. They had no lusts or whims. They were eviscerated. James got his famous unity by omitting mentions of all that was vital in life.

Having first made sure that he has scarcely anything left to express, he then sets to work to express it, with an industry, a wealth of intellectual stuff that dwarfs Newton. He spares no resource in the telling of his dead inventions. . . . His vast paragraphs sweat and struggle; they could not sweat and elbow and struggle more if God Himself was the processional meaning to which they sought to come. And all for tales of nothingness. . . . It is leviathan retrieving pebbles. It is a magnificent but painful hippopotamus resolved at any cost, even at the cost of its dignity, upon picking up a pea which has got into a corner of its den.

Uninhibited by the background and character which would have made such antics impossible for his victim, Wells parodied James's style. He burlesqued his method with a story set in "Samphire House." He reached the apex of his ridicule with this description of a James novel: ". . . church lit but without a congregation to distract you, with every light and line focussed on the high altar. And on the altar, very reverently placed, intensely there, is a dead kitten, an egg-shell, a bit of string."

Delighted with his effort, Wells left a copy of *Boon* at his club for Henry James. Stunned at first, James was deeply hurt. He wrote Wells with dignity regretting that their friendship must end. There were replies and re-replies, but there was no reconciliation. Aged seventy-two, James died two years later.

11

Soon after the publication of *Boon* the world had no time at all for literary dispute. The World War (it was *the* world war then, not just the first installment in a continuing series) broke out in August 1914.

H. G. Wells had been prophesying world conflict for years. He had envisioned aerial warfare and the use of tanks. He had foreseen total war involving civilians as well as the military. When Louis Blériot flew across the English Channel from France in 1909, Wells was convinced that England could easily be invaded from the air. That same year, writing in the New York *World* he had talked of huge, destructive war made more deadly by the use of balloons and planes. He had described modern war as "an insanity, not a sane business proposition." Early in 1914 in a novel called *The World Set Free* he had prophesied use of the atomic bomb in world conflict. Made with an element called "Carolinium," it would be dropped in 1958. Wells called the atom bomb correctly and missed the date by only a dozen years.

Wells had tried to warn the world, yet when war came

he was as stunned, as incredulous, and as indignant as everyone else. He had lived in a world of peace, of ideas, a world ruled largely by Great Britain in which it was safe to talk about war and to demand social revolution.

Suddenly all the peace and security were gone. The Allies were in murderous conflict with the Central Powers on a scale which even Wells had thought improbable. The apostle of socialism and one world was thrown into an agony of nationalistic patriotism as Germany overran Belgium and invaded France. He plunged into a maelstrom of journalistic activities. He kept on prophesying—he could never help it—but the actualities of murderous gunfire just across the Channel, of millions of young men dying in the trenches, of the mass drownings at sea as great ships were sunk without warning by German submarines demanded action, and Wells responded furiously.

He blamed Prussian imperialism for the war. He called for annihilation of the Hohenzollern rulers of Germany. He demanded ten thousand airplanes for the mass bombing of German industry. In newspaper diatribes that were later gathered into ephemeral books he cried out against the "Boche" and the "Huns."

Some of his friends and associates, like Bertrand Russell, were aghast. They felt that Wells had deserted the cause of pacificism and socialism to which they remained loyal. Wells did not see it that way. Seized by a patriotic fervor which may have surprised him, he rationalized away any inconsistencies of which he was accused and threw himself into writing the war out of existence.

Like most people, he thought at first that the war would

*H. G. Wells visiting the Western Front
near Soissons, France, during World War I.*

end quickly. He made prophecies about it which proved no wiser than the hopes and guesses of other men. Like other well-known and influential journalists, he was sent to see the Allied armies in action so that knowledge of the actualities would make his denunciations of the Kaiser and Krupp, the German munitions maker, even fiercer. In the summer of 1916 he inspected the Italian and French fronts. He had an interview with Marshal Joffre, the French commander-in-chief. He inspected both the British and French facilities for aerial photography. With C. E. Montague of the *Manchester Guardian* as his reckless guide, he penetrated briefly to the front lines where in stalemated trench warfare the Allies faced the German forces across "No Man's Land."

With Winston Churchill, who in the end was responsible for their construction and use toward the close of the war, Wells pled for tanks, long derided by the military. He persuaded the reluctant authorities to build and try out a device he conceived for getting supplies and equipment to the front line trenches without soldiers having to carry them on their backs through the mud and slime.

Wells's chief war service, though, was in propaganda. He invented the phrase which is still tagged, ironically now, to World War I. It was "the war to end war." Propaganda, persuasion through words to convince a nation of the righteousness of its cause and to confuse and delude the enemy, was used consciously as a weapon for the first time in World War I. A Ministry of Propaganda was set up under Lord Northcliffe, now as publisher of *The Times* the press power in England. Wells's friend Arnold

Bennett worked hard in this ministry. Northcliffe appointed Wells to conduct all of the propaganda against Germany.

Wells helped to create and plan the distribution of pamphlets, dropped by planes or circulated by secret agents, to show the German people the evil and the hopelessness of their cause. He helped maintain morale in Britain. Duplicity, half truths, and lies were part of this warfare of words. They always are.

Wells tried to go further. He urged that the Allies make open statement of their war aims. He and a colleague in the Ministry of Propaganda prepared a statement. They tried hard to get it approved and released. The English Foreign Office balked their attempts.

Wells had no illusions about the politicians, diplomats, and military staff officers with whom he tried to work. He considered them incapable and devious. They were low-grade idiots who had received their only lasting education from their governesses. He soon lost any other illusions he might have had about their intelligence and their conduct of the war.

More than twenty years later he was still bitter about it. Just before the outbreak of another world conflict which he had prophesied he told the P.E.N. Club, of which he was then president,

> We were kept in the dark about all sorts of secret entanglements to which these gentry had committed the country, and we were allowed to hold out hopes to the German people of a liberal postwar settlement

our masters had no intention of making. We were tricked and, through us, the German liberals were cheated, and what these tricksters of the British Foreign Office and the Quai d'Orsay imagined they were doing except being very, very diplomatic and very clever about their double-crossing and generally having the laugh of their betters, I cannot imagine. Betters, I say without a blush. Every disastrous thing that has happened in the past twenty years was clearly foretold by a galaxy of writers and thinkers twenty years ago. Our politicians and officials were, relatively speaking, little, purblind, mean chaps. Orders and titles cannot alter that. It filled them with joy to snub the highbrows. The evil state of Europe today is traceable almost directly to the want of imagination, the self-protective cunning, and the deliberate breaches of faith made by them during the eventful years that immediately followed the Great War.

Wells spilled out propaganda and journalistic books during World War I, but wrote only one book that has lasted. It was immensely popular after its publication in 1916. It became one of the outstanding novels of the war and is still read. The novel was *Mr. Britling Sees It Through.*

It is fictional autobiography shaped, formed, and embroidered to give a picture of a man physically, mentally, and morally much like H. G. Wells and of his thoughts and actions, and of those close to him and like him, during the early years of the war to end war.

Mr. Britling, thinker and writer of some eminence, lives in the Dower House of Claverings Park in the Essex countryside. He has a wife and two young sons. They and the happy, haphazard house at Matching's Easy are inundated by a turmoil of guests and attendants. There is a German tutor, a secretary and her sister with a husband and baby, a visiting American, and an unassorted lot of other young people. They live in a riot of work, hockey, charades, visiting, and talk.

This is Mr. Britling's second marriage, and he is enjoying or harassed by his eighth love affair. "A man of lively imagination and quick impulses naturally has love affairs as he drives through life, just as he naturally has accidents if he drives an automobile."

At first the silly little war in the Balkans does not seriously interfere with either the love affair or the happy helter-skelter of life at Matching's Easy. Too quickly it does. Herr Heinrich, the German tutor, blond, plump, bespectacled, is called back to Germany for army service. He goes puzzled and unwilling. Other young men about the Dower House enlist. More go off from the village. Though he is not yet nineteen, Mr. Britling's older son, Hugh, enlists.

Perturbed and confused, Mr. Britling writes his newspaper and magazine articles at night. He tries to extract what meaning he can from the initial astonishment to the resentfully settling down to the long and bitter struggle. He and other civilized men feel a tragic disillusionment and the dull pain of disappointed hopes and mounting fears.

Wells considered *Mr. Britling* one of the best of his novels, and it is. It is because the people in this story of the actual and paining present feel as well as think. They hope. They suffer and endure. They try to comfort each other. Yet Wells could not, of course, wholly neglect his mission and his message. Mr. Britling, grieving for the death of his son killed in France, is talking to Letty, grieving for her husband, supposedly killed in action. Only a better world could prevent recurrence of the folly and the horror, the war in which millions of young men were being maimed or murdered.

> . . . the great republic of the united states of the world must keep the federal peace. . . . That's the plain sense of life; the federal world-republic. Why do we bother ourselves with loyalties to any other government but that? It needs only that sufficient men should say it, and that republic would be here now. Why have we loitered so long—until these tragic punishments come?

Mr. Britling knew that "In the end this world-republic, this sane government of the world, is as certain as the sunset."

Near the end of the book, stunned by Hugh's death, Mr. Britling sits down to write to the father of Heinrich, who had been killed fighting for Germany. The young of the world were being uselessly slaughtered. All Europe was ablaze. In the midst of it all one bereaved father tried to write another suffering man, whom he had never met, what words of consolation he could manage. It is a human and touching scene.

In the letter he tried to write, Mr. Britling found himself seeking reassurance in God. "And for the first time clearly he felt a Presence of which he had thought very many times in the last few weeks, a Presence so close to him that it was behind his eyes and in his brain and hands. . . . it was Hugh . . . it was young Heinrich . . . it was those others that sought . . . it was the Master, the Captain of Mankind, it was God, there present with him, and he knew that it was God. . . . God was beside him and within him and about him. . . . It was the crucial moment of Mr. Britling's life."

The emotion betrayed in this scene gripped the imagination of Wells's readers. They felt what Mr. Britling felt. Wells expressed for them what they could not say. People wrote Wells expressions of sympathy over the loss of his son. Wells lost no son in the World War, but he had been so convincing that people thought he had suffered as many of them had suffered.

It took Wells some time and several new books to explain away this seeming apostasy from atheism. He said he had not meant the conventional God. He had forsworn none of his disbeliefs. He said finally that by "God" he had meant a deification of human courage.

Mr. Britling was read avidly in the United States, which not yet in the war was strongly pro-Ally. The book brought H. G. Wells about a hundred thousand dollars in profit from its sales in this country alone. Though he did not intend it as such, *Mr. Britling* was the best wartime propaganda he wrote.

Wells hoped the war would mean the breakup of the

capitalistic system. He had hoped that the evil and de-structiveness would in the end produce a universal good. In one of his London newspaper articles he wrote: "Now is the opportunity to do fundamental things that will not otherwise get done for hundreds of years. If Liberals throughout the world . . . will insist upon a World con-ference at the end of this conflict, if they will refuse all partial settlements and merely European solutions, they may re-draw every frontier they choose, they may reduce a thousand chafing conflicts of race and language and government to a minimum, and set up a Peace League that will control the globe."

The idea of a global union of nations had been for-warded in England some years earlier. A League of Na-tions Society had been formed in 1915. Wells backed it strenuously. He helped form all the organizations founded to promote the League into a League of Nations Union. He wrote articles and pamphlets advocating the League of Nations.

Wells considered President Woodrow Wilson narrow, uninformed, and self-righteous. Yet, through Bainbridge Colby—Wilson's law partner and adviser, later Secretary of State—he wrote a long letter to him urging that the United States take the lead in establishing the League of Nations with Wilson the one man able to bring about the reality. Wilson's long and losing fight for the League is, of course, part of history now.

When Wilson and the other political leaders of the victorious Allies gathered to create the Treaty of Ver-sailles, Wells's disillusionment with the peace they concocted and the League of Nations that emerged from the peace conference in January 1920 was complete. He felt that he and other intellectuals had been abysmally betrayed, and abandoning all hope for the peace and for the League, turned his attention elsewhere.

If men could not or would not see what was necessary for the salvation of the world, Wells would make them see. Single-handedly—it seems a measure of both his conceit and his courage that it was the way in which Wells always had to work—he decided to solve the world's problems through a different attack. Actually, he had already begun.

12

H. G. Wells felt that men did not understand the present and the demands of the future because they did not understand the past. He felt confident that he did understand it. With all his boundless energy and determination he set about correcting the situation.

When he sat in the Tower of London waiting to be beheaded, Sir Walter Raleigh began to write the *History of the World*. He completed only one volume before he was executed. Though he knew he risked beheading by the axes of professional historians and academic critics, H. G. Wells decided he would write his own history of the world.

He despised history taught as patriotism in the schools, history written and promoted for nationalistic purposes. He wanted to put down the whole history of mankind, as he thought it was, from the beginning of plant and animal life to the year in which he wrote. At first he intended only a long essay showing that all history is the record of man's progress through forming associations and federations. He tried to enlist established historians in the enterprise that grew as he worked on it.

Fearful of the grandiosity of a scheme that only an amateur could have dreamed up or would attempt, they would have none of H. G. Wells and his project. They would be risking their reputations as scholars. They would fall victim to the ridicule that unfailingly would fall on any school or university teacher who attempted so impossible a subject.

Wells thereupon decided to do the whole job himself. He knew something of botany and zoölogy. He felt he knew something of the other natural and social sciences. With the *Encyclopedia Britannica* as guide, he struggled to fill the gaps in his knowledge and to tie everything together into some kind of a whole.

Even H. G. Wells knew that he was undertaking a formidable task. He and his wife checked their finances to decide how long he could afford to stay out of the public eye as novelist and journalist. He gathered a small staff of specialists, not to help write his history, but to guide him in his reading and to read what he wrote. The staff included Gilbert Murray, Philip Guedella, Sir Harry Johnson, and Sir Denison Ross.

Wells knew he had a mind particularly adapted to the making of outlines. This would be the largest outline he had ever attempted. Characteristically he completed the huge job in about a year's time. *The Outline of History* by H. G. Wells was published, first in parts, then as a huge complete book, in London in 1920. Doubtful of possible sales, an American publisher took it on with some reluctance. The *Outline* was immediately a runaway bestseller. It became the first postwar publishing sensation in England and in this country.

Wells had intended the book as a school and college text. He believed that only through education could the world be saved, and this was to be his contribution to the proper teaching and understanding of history as a first step toward that salvation. He should have known his schoolmasters and professors better. Educators either ignored or condemned the *Outline*. It had not come out of the established tradition under the proper academic auspices. They also thought—and they were correct— that Wells went to history not as a student or a scholar investigating the past but as a journalist who wrote in sweeping generalizations to support a priori convictions.

Intellectuals who were not of Wells's socialistic persuasions spurned the book. In his autobiographical *Georgian Adventure*, Douglas Jerrold refers to "Mr. H. G. Wells, who, on the somewhat slender foundation of a thigh-bone or two, can write the detailed life-story, accompanied by full-length portraits, of all our prehistoric ancestors, together with an exhaustive account of their social and political ambitions, their repressions, complexes, and even their love-life." Jerrold's irony was deserved. One unfriendly critic wrote that Wells was simply continuing his education in public.

It was not the schools or the scholars who took to the *Outline* but the general public. A long war had left people tired and baffled. They wanted to know how it had happened and why it would or would not happen again. They had been forced to learn something of the outside world. They wanted to know more. They wanted life and the world explained, and here was a possible explanation. People bought *The Outline of History* in carload lots.

Two million copies were sold in the United States alone. The *Outline* was translated into many foreign languages. Wells, who had been well-to-do before, became wealthy.

The Outline of History was encyclopedic. Often it was prosaic, and often it was bare, but it was simple and it was clear. The facts were accurate. To real historians history is not that simple and it is not that clear. Its facts are often debatable, and interpretation of those facts difficult. Scholars objected also because the *Outline* was obviously and admittedly thesis history. That was just what Wells intended: history so arranged as to show the inevitability of human progress which would have to culminate in world federation.

Whether they agreed with his thesis or even noticed it, people relished the *Outline*. It was story. It was readable, reasonable, and understandable. It placed them in time and restored some of their shaken faith in themselves and the world. To many the *Outline* in its two volumes was not, as it was to the historian, meager and elementary, but rich and full.

Wells later revised his work several times, even shortened it into the more compact *A Short History of the World*. He had encompassed almost the whole of everything now, but not quite. He planned an outline of biology. With work by his older son, who was a biologist, and Julian Huxley, it appeared in 1930 as *The Science of Life*. He wrote an outline of the social sciences which he published as *The Work, Wealth, and Happiness of Mankind*. Neither of these attained anything like the popularity of his *Outline of History*.

In 1920, drawn by the spectacle of the new social order being created there after the Bolshevik Revolution of 1917, Wells went again to Russia. The huge country had thrown off its past and was beginning anew. It had to rebuild from scratch. It had abandoned private enterprise and traditional religion for collectivism, state control, and the scientific approach to a national existence. In theory this was all that Wells approved. There was even the possibility that a brave new world could emerge in the Soviet.

Wells saw the desolation in Russia. The little shops that he had liked were all closed. The bad roads were filled with shell holes. The population of St. Petersburg had fallen from 1,200,000 to about 700,000. Streetcars ran only until six o'clock in the evening. Any automobiles that had survived the street warfare of the Revolution were running on kerosene. Food was rationed. Drugs were unobtainable. Clothing was scarce. Even the novelist and playwright Maxim Gorky, the friend with whom Wells stayed, possessed only one suit of clothes.

In Moscow, Wells talked at length with Lenin, leader of the Bolshevik Revolution and first head of the U.S.S.R. They discussed the planned electrification of Russia, large-scale collective farming, and other programs which later became the first of the five-year plans for the industrial and economic development of the Soviet Union. Lenin asked when the socialist revolution would take place in England. Wells explained that he was neither a Marxist nor a communist but a state socialist. Wells had always distrusted the Marxist theory of the class struggle

—the proletariat of the workers against the commercial and wealth-owning *bourgeoisie*—but he admired Lenin's adaptation of Marxism. Interpreting Marx liberally, Lenin was using private enterprise in part to help rebuild the badly disorganized Bolshevik state. Wells saw Lenin as intelligent and aggressive, a capable planner working against great obstacles with zeal and skill.

When he returned to England, Wells talked with British government leaders. He urged that, despite disapproval of communism, England help the weak and struggling U.S.S.R. with manufactured products and technical help. He was not heeded, and Wells fumed anew at what he continued to call the governess-trained official mind.

Wells had planned a lecture tour of the United States for the fall of 1920 but illness prevented his going. Instead he published the material he had already prepared. He urged adoption of the world state instead of trying to strengthen the weak League of Nations. He pled for general education by means of large outlines, such as he had written, of history, science, and the like. He insisted that the place to get a sound general education was where the thing was being done. This is vague, but Wells was usually vague. He was the persistent salesman, the exhorting evangelist. A world executive on the largest possible scale, the little generalizer advised on policy only, not on operational procedures.

A year later Wells did return to the United States. He came to cover the Washington Disarmament Conference in 1921 for the New York *World*. Instead of seeming just another foreign correspondent, he seemed more like another world figure among all those gathered for a meeting which it was hoped would produce important and conclusive results. Wells was prophet, pundit, and untiring propagandist for his world state. He was the author of *Mr. Britling*, which so many Americans had read. He was the man of the future and the master historian of the past. He was the very visible and vocal creator of the invisible man.

Despite valiant attempts, the Washington conferees could not reach general agreement on limitations of land armament. They did agree to limit construction of capital ships—battleships—for ten years. England, the United States, France, Italy, and Japan could then add battleships to their fleets by fixed ratio. No restrictions were placed on the construction of small naval craft, cruisers, destroyers, etc. The conferees dispersed feeling that some progress toward world peace had been made, but H .G. Wells saw no advance toward his cherished world state.

He was becoming impatient and incensed. In book after book, pamphlet after tractarian pamphlet, he fought for the world state and threatened disaster if it were not created forthwith. He wrote syndicated newspaper articles, gathered in 1924 in *A Year of Prophesying*, on the political situations in France, England, and Germany. He attacked the lack of liberalism in Germany and French occupation of the industrial Ruhr Valley. In a novel, *Meanwhile* (1927), he was to attack Fascism and ridicule Mussolini. "One need only to study a few of the innumerable photographs of Mussolini with which the world is now bespattered to realize that he is a resultant and no original. That round, forcible-feeble face is the popular actor's face in perfection. It stares, usually out of some pseudo-heroic costume, under a helmet for choice, with eyes devoid of thought or intelligence and an expression of vacuous challenge."

In 1923 the sharp-eyed reporter of contemporary politics took refuge once more in the future. He went back to utopia in *Men Like Gods*. He had changed his mind about some things. He saw no voluntary aristocratic class of Samurai now. In the introduction which he wrote for this book in the Atlantic Edition of his works he stated: ". . . all the people are Samurai. The writer's belief in a scientific reorganization of society based on a broader conception of education has grown more confident with the years. He is no longer disposed to admit the necessary survival of inferior types."

There was another change. In *Men Like Gods* nobody wears clothes. Wells admitted that this nudity posed some problems for the book's illustrator but for him it symbolized "that stark reality which is the very soul of the new world of the author's belief and desire." In his new world there would be no taboos, no "restraints or disguises," no clothes. It seems not to have occurred to Wells that the inhabitants of utopia might feel rather chilly.

Wells always prided himself upon being a Cockney: sharp, impudent, indomitable. Mr. Polly never minded calling rival shopkeepers names while he was out sweeping his sidewalk. George Ponderevo, Remington, certainly George Boon, enjoyed being derisive. Wells himself always felt free to ridicule his enemies. He was beginning to show another cockney characteristic. The Cockney often becomes a scold, and Wells was not far from it in the introduction to *Men Like Gods*.

People were paying too little attention to his directions, admonitions, and repeated adjurations, and he was getting a little tired of their neglect. Some people, he admitted, might feel uncomfortable in the utopia he pictured—". . . just as a rat-infested drain is richer in interest for a dog than a library or a laboratory."

13

A journalist, always on the lookout for a story or an idea which he could work up into salable copy, H. G. Wells found a superabundance of material for his articles and books as he lived along.

Every experience, everything he observed, became the possibility of a book, and usually he turned the possibility into an actuality, especially when the subject was of compelling interest to him. There had come the point when he had to see to the formal education of his two sons. Like parents before and since, he went about investigating. In his search he came upon a school which seemed to fit most of his requirements and a schoolmaster who provoked his lasting admiration. He settled on Oundle School for his sons and F. W. Sanderson, its head, for his nearly ideal schoolmaster.

Out of the whole, of course, came a new novel. *Joan and Peter* (1918) is subtitled "the story of an education."

The novel is nearly six hundred pages long. It is formless. It is disordered or unordered. In the guise of fiction it is a polemic on education and everything that seems connected with it, and most things are. Its hero, Oswald Sydenham, becomes one of the guardians of Joan and Peter after the death of their parents in a boating mishap. Sydenham is a naval hero with a Victoria Cross and a badly scarred face, an African explorer, a manly man of the British Empire straight out of Kipling or one of the adventure stories of John Buchan. He had also, of course, studied biology under Thomas Henry Huxley.

Wells could not depict children. His baby talk is grotesque, and his sentimental humor in *Joan and Peter* is labored. His description of the mismanaged education of the two children until Oswald seriously takes charge of it becomes as tedious as his indignation is marked. Wells was writing another encyclopedic essay on education, war, peace, women, Catholicism, the teaching of sex, and the stupidity of teaching Latin and Greek. Didactic and schoolteacherish as he so often was, he pled for the factual and the practical in education.

The characters in *Joan and Peter* talk in essays. Their dialogue is dialectic. Peter, who goes finally to Cambridge and then into the Royal Air Corps during World War I, emerges as manly-heroic as Oswald. Joan becomes the same bright "new woman," a liberalized lady, who appears in so many of Wells's novels.

Even Wells considered *Joan and Peter* unsatisfactory, but under the compulsion that drove him he had always to say what he had to say. Each time—after each book— he must have felt, "This time I've done it." Each time he became dissatisfied after a time and had to try again.

He would exult as he worked along on the new book

in which this time he would really get it all said, finish it with a feeling of triumph, then discover once more how far short he had fallen of the accomplishment he intended. In his autobiography he tells how he kept making fresh starts in life. Each book was likewise a fresh start at remaking life for everyone in it. His enthusiasm and his vigor did not wane. They seemed to gain in force with each attempt. Because his temperament would not let him, he could not stop trying. That is one of the most engaging things about H. G. Wells.

He seemed never to tire. Yet he did tire in the early 1920s. He wanted to get away, to regroup his force for new attack. It was planned retreat before a stronger offensive. Like Remington in *The New Machiavelli*, he withdrew to the Continent. Like many other English writers he took refuge on the French Riviera.

He maintained his permanent home in Easton Glebe but in 1924, after first flying to Geneva to attend an assembly of the League of Nations, he abandoned plans for an around-the-world trip and found a country retreat near Grasse. Later he built a house, Lou Pidou, complete with terraces, gardens, rose beds, and the other amenities of country life in the south of France.

At Grasse, Wells spent three winters thinking and writing. The result this time was a two-volume novel, *The World of William Clissold* (1926). Wells considered it an important book. It was published and reviewed by the critics as an important book. Once more, it was hardly a novel in anything but its fictional frame. If *The New Machiavelli* and *Joan and Peter* had been discursive, *The*

World of William Clissold was extravagantly wide-ranging.

This time Wells cast himself in a new and even more glamorous role. He became a retired industrialist on the largest scale. The 1920s was the decade of Big Business and the Big Businessman dealing almost casually with flocks of industries, vast sums of money, cartels, international monopolies. The industrialist was a romantic figure.

Including "A Note before the Title Page," *The World of William Clissold* runs to just over eight hundred pages. In this prefatory note, Wells insisted that it was a novel and nothing more. Obviously this shrill declaration was protest in advance against attacks he knew the book would provoke. He insisted that William Clissold was a fictitious character and not the author. Everybody who had ever identified him with one of his heroes was mistaken. People who had identified Mr. Britling's Dower House with Easton Glebe were mistaken. All the other characters, except those mentioned by name, in *The World of William Clissold* were fictitious.

In the novel Wells mentioned Woodrow Wilson, the Swiss psychiatrist Carl Jung, the British economist John Maynard Keynes, the American-born London merchant Harry Gordon Selfridge, and other public figures. Wells even introduced and discussed H. G. Wells, identifying him as a distant cousin of the author.

Clissold is verbose. Wells spends many chapters introducing William Clissold and his brother Dickon, and many chapters describing his Riviera home and his life in it. *Clissold* is very slow getting under way, and slow all the way through. Clissold or Wells reflects on socialism v. capitalism, sex, Karl Marx, death, Edmund Gosse, patent medicines, education, morality, journalism, universities, advertising . . .

Advertising seems to have fascinated Wells. He could not let it alone. In *Tono-Bungay* he ridiculed advertising and its excesses. In *Clissold* he makes Dickon, admiringly, an advertising genius, the greatest advertising man of his time. Dickon conceived of advertising as a way of promoting ideas as well as products. This advertising was a powerful instrument for public education and social good.

. . . Slums, race prejudice, liberalism, the art of being a rake, birth control—Wells seems to cover everything in a book so contemporary that whole chunks of it read like the reporting and discussion in news magazines. Though the description sounds contradictory, *Clissold* is a monumental muddle of clear-eyed, hard-brained journalism.

Yet the book has one central idea. Wells was selling his world state again, but this time advocating its establishment through a different means.

Once he had envisaged the possibility of making his united states of the world an actuality via the far-flung British Empire. For a time he had hoped to bring it about through Fabianism. He had stood as a Labor Party candidate for Parliament in 1922 and 1923 in the hope that Labor could make the world state a reality. He had fought early for a League of Nations that would be a world state. All of these avenues had failed him.

He turned now to the internationalism of industry.

Business, with interests and investments, often plants and offices, on several continents and in many countries was already a kind of industrial world state. It could grow, develop, and become a world-wide republic. What Wells through William Clissold advocated was an "Open Conspiracy."

In *Tono-Bungay* the businessman was represented as sinfully selfseeking. In *Clissold* he is the possible savior of mankind. Those who control industry, finance, and communications are the real revolutionists. Through building an international network of corporate enterprises, of primary and supporting manufacturing and distributing organizations, they had formed an economic world state. If they joined forces with the scientists, they could improve the living conditions of humanity everywhere. In short, with his "Open Conspiracy," Wells looked for the coming of the world state not through political or military action but through the natural international activities of business allied to science and propaganda.

The prophet had ceased prophesying for a time to deal with realities. He found them among a segment of the population which previously he would credit with neither intelligence nor good will. William and Dickon Clissold would be charter members of this new Samurai. Those who followed them in this world elite would have even greater vision leading to greater accomplishments.

Wells lectured on his new idea at the Sorbonne in Paris later that year. Amy Catherine Wells was with him. She died in 1927. Wells went alone to speak at the *Reichstag* in Berlin, then to talk about his world conspiracy in Madrid, Oxford, and the United States. He wrote about his new conspiracy in newspaper and magazine articles and clamored for internationalism in books under a half-dozen new titles. He traveled far afield to inspect sweeping political and social changes he felt promised accomplishment he approved.

In 1934 he came to the United States to examine the New Deal, inaugurated two years earlier by President Franklin D. Roosevelt. He was famous. He was entertained. He talked to many who had opinions for or against the sweeping changes, the welfare programs, and the social planning originated by Roosevelt and his advisers and implemented by his administration.

Wells found men enthusiastically for or bitterly against the reformation. Some, like his old friend Clarence Darrow, clung to the right of the individual to be free, to go his own way, do his own work, live his own life. Others, like Roosevelt himself, disparaged the once admired "rugged individualism" which they blamed for the economic and social ills of the time and worked to stamp out. They lauded the new controlled society they were bringing into being. Wells listened without admiration to Father Coughlin, then a popular radio commentator. In the Senate Office Building he talked with Huey Long and commented on the mental crudity of the Louisiana Senator.

At the White House for the fourth time to talk with an American President, Wells was as impressed by Franklin D. Roosevelt as he had been by Theodore Roosevelt.

BROWN BROTHERS

H. G. Wells arriving in New York.

Man of the hour, FDR was the architect of a socialized state after Wells's own heart. In *Fate of Man* Wells said, "His New Deal involves such collective controls of the national business that it would be absurd to call it anything but socialism, were it not for a prejudice lingering on from the old individualistic days against the word."

Wells—at first—was almost equally impressed by the Brain Trust, that now almost forgotten chorus of the early days of the New Deal. Roosevelt had gathered intellectuals about him, appointing economists, social scientists, and other university professors to posts in his administration. They were to provide him with the best objective thinking of the time on social planning and to help administer the programs they suggested and he approved. Wells saw this as the ideal situation. A socialistic government was drawing on the best brains of the nation to create a new state.

Later his early enthusiasm for President Roosevelt and for the Brain Trust waned. He began to see FDR as well intentioned, intent on creating a scientifically organized socialized state, but not deeply involved in it himself. Because of his wealth he was a patrician. This and his physical disability kept him a level above daily concerns. He relegated important matters to subordinates. Many of these were the Brain Trusters, who by this time were off riding their own hobby horses and jockeying for position and preference. Reasonably and moderately, Wells decided that the Brain Trust was "a collection of oddities."

In July of this same year, accompanied by his biologist

son who had studied Russian at Oundle, H. G. Wells returned to Russia.

Well in advance of most people Wells saw that the United States and Soviet Russia were emerging as world leaders. In both countries significant social and political changes had occurred. Fresh from his talks with Roosevelt, Wells wanted to talk with his counterpart. He wanted to talk with Russia's dictator about the possibilities of basic understanding and cooperation between the English-speaking and the Russian-speaking communities which could result in world organization.

Stalin greeted him cordially, smoking his pipe while he and Wells talked for three hours in the Kremlin. Stalin seemed candid and unaffected, but it did not take Wells long to discover that he was rigid in his adherence to Marxism and the Moscow party line. Stalin could not conceive of anything but proletarian communism and the necessity and inevitability of its dominating the world. There was no room for argument or even for discussion.

Stalin knew that the Soviet system was the only possible system. Changes in the United States mattered no more to Russia than the lack of significant change in England. He could not conceive of a world state along the lines Wells suggested. The U.S.S.R. was replete with the same kind of nationalism and nationalistic pride that Wells decried everywhere. He felt completely frustrated.

All during the ten days he spent in Russia, Wells saw building, rebuilding, and expansion. He told of unco-ordinated plans for still more and more construction. He was shocked at the change in his friend Gorky. Now a literary hero of the Soviet, living in palatial quarters awarded him by the state, Gorky adhered as closely as Stalin to the Marxist line. His liberalism was as gone as if it had never been.

Only when Wells and his biologist son visited the eighty-five-year-old Ivan Pavlov at his Institute for Psychological Research near Leningrad did Wells find anything that he could recognize with pleasure. The world-famed physiologist paid small attention to communist political theory. He went to church as he had always done. He had a governess for his two small grandchildren. He insisted on the need for complete intellectual freedom in science and dismissed the rest of Marxist U.S.S.R. from his mind.

There was some liberal feeling and agreement among the writers to whom Wells talked in the home of Alexis Tolstoy. They agreed, in theory at any rate, with Wells's proposal of an association to promote the freedom of scientific thought and artistic expression throughout the world.

Wells was sixty-eight when he visited the United States and Russia in 1934. He was a wealthy and established writer who after the death of his wife had sold both Easton Glebe and Lou Pidou. He lived well in a flat in fashionable London. His eminence had been recognized four years before in a full-length biography by Geoffrey West (his real name Wells, but not a relative).

Wells had given his biographer all the factual help he could, corrected the manuscript, and written an introduction to the book. In it he had disclaimed pretence to being a serious literary artist, said he knew that much of his writing had been of only temporary value, and described himself amusingly as "a haphazard and pampered prophet." Wells approved West's book, calling it an exact and careful biography, but evidently it only whetted his appetite for more. He began his autobiography.

Wells knew his subject well. He had been writing about it for years. This time he wrote about himself openly in a book three times as large as West's official biography. In 1934 he published *Experiment in Autobiography*. With the mock modesty he often disparaged in others, he subtitled it "Discoveries and Conclusions of a Very Ordinary Brain (Since 1866)."

The *Experiment in Autobiography* is a vast, rambling, disconnected book. It is a candid, provocative, sharply written book. Wells, who had always been articulate, had become voluble in his early books, verbose in *Joan and Peter*, garrulous in *The World of William Clissold*. The *Autobiography* is hardly laconic. Replete with frank memories, charitable and uncharitable character sketches, overflowing with science, socialism, and reiterated pleading for his consuming idea, it is confident, dogmatic, informative Wellsian talk.

Often publication of a biography or an autobiography marks the end of a man's career. Publication of both should insure it. There was too much life in H. G. Wells for that. In 1921 Wells had published a slight book called *The Salvaging of Civilization*. He kept right on trying to salvage it.

14

In an essay appended to early editions of his *Outline of History* H. G. Wells declared: "Human history becomes more and more a race between education and catastrophe."

With Wells education was not an interest. It was an obsession. His early experiences as a student of teaching methods and as a secondary-school teacher had made him not an educator but an outspoken antagonist of ordinary schooling and opponent of ordinary teachers. Henry Seidel Canby, professor of English at Yale and formative editor of *The Saturday Review of Literature* (now the *Saturday Review*), spoke gleefully of Wells's "slaughter" (no milder term will suffice) "of professional educators" in his autobiography.

Wells, who had come to look on education as a cure for most of the ills of society, had strong ideas as to how it should be changed. It should be science-oriented, as his own had been. Everyone should go to school until age sixteen, then continue with some kind of studies for another three years. At first scornful of Latin and Greek,

Wells decided that together with a sound knowledge of history and science and thorough training in English, the student should have some acquaintance with the classical languages. Education should teach the student how to use his body and his brain.

For him, Wells became quite specific in a paper, "The Formative Content of Education," which he read as the presidential address to the Educational Science Section of the British Association for the Advancement of Science at Nottingham, September 12, 1937.

Wells said that as an outsider he could talk freely. He meant that if he offended an administrator or pedagogical expert—there are many more now than when he spoke— he could not be fired. He said, too, that he was talking of the irreducible minimum in basic education as preparation for modern life. He was blunt.

> Many of our teachers—and I am not speaking only of elementary schools—are shockingly illiterate and ignorant. Often they know nothing but school subjects; sometimes they scarcely know them.

Strongly organized and always sensitive to any hint of unfavorable criticism, teachers today would like the comment no better than did those who heard Wells speak or read his words.

Wells advocated the use of films, photography, and visual aids in teaching. He advised teaching young children local topography as a basis for geography. They should be taught zoölogy from observation of animals and botany from the plant life around them. History should be taught so as to show that the world is one community.

Wells wished older children taught not just one religion and one kind of morality but about all religions and
moral systems. He asked that education continue into
adult life, citing again the intellectual staleness of most
middle-aged professional people, including teachers.

The universities should be made centers of thought and
research. They should become again what universities
had been originally, a group of scholars who attracted advanced students. Even when he descended to specifics,
H. G. Wells could not help thinking a little larger than
large. The author of *The Outline of History* asked a
world encyclopedia organization to organize and diagram
all knowledge for teaching all the world.

Wells was scolded for his blunt words in Nottingham.
Teachers expressed their displeasure, some their disgust.
Wells defended himself in "Ruffled Teachers," an article
in the *Sunday Chronicle*. "I should hate to think it is true
that you can teach something to every man (or woman)
except a schoolmaster (or schoolmistress)."

Much of Wells's insistence on educational improvement, as his plea for socialism, stemmed from chronic resentment at what he considered the unfair handicap of
his birth and upbringing. Most successful men manage to
forget, at least to forgive, what humble beginnings they
may have had to overcome. Wells never forgot, and he
never forgave.

Geoffrey West had told his life story. Wells had
written his full-to-overflowing autobiography, but these
did not suffice. Never handicapped by undue modesty,
he returned to the autobiographical in an introduction to
The Fate of Man (1939). He complained again of his

early experiences. He had been given old books to read. He had been taught old and false religious values. He had been inadequately taught at school. He had had his social inferiority borne in upon him as part of the fixed social order, and he had hated it. He had been "thrust into the hopeless drudgery of a shop, ignorant, misinformed, undernourished, and physically underdeveloped, without warning and without guidance, at the age of thirteen."

In *The Fate of Man*, some of it drawn from lectures he gave in the United States in 1937, Wells repeated his old charges against the world and urged the causes for which he had battled for so long. He attacked the universities for not doing their proper job, spoke of his disappointment with Roosevelt and the Brain Trust, dispatched "the Jewish Problem," and attacked Catholicism again for being what he considered a reactionary institution. Men lived in a decadent world. They would have to adapt themselves to changed conditions.

In *The Fate of Man* Wells also prophesied the second world war. He promised that it would bring about a collapse of civilization and a new barbarism. He was so often right.

The war that he foresaw came very quickly. Wells called Adolf Hitler a lunatic and said that he should be certified insane and institutionalized, but he had learned his lesson well in the first world war. Wells was not led into any fervor of nationalistic patriotism or unthinking loyalty to a new Allied cause. He wrote no propaganda. Instead, he said what he thought.

An Associated Press article, datelined New York, February 17, 1940, was given front-page prominence in many American newspapers when Wells, whom it quoted as "the great English historian," published his *New World Order*. In the book Wells said that Great Britain was fighting because of its ruling class's fear of change. He could see no fundamental difference between the totalitarian countries of Russia, Italy, and Germany, and the rest of the world.

Wells had no concern with the embattled nations. His concern was for man. He offered what he called a "Declaration of the Rights of Man." By right of birth everyone should be entitled to food, medical care, and a full education. He should be entitled to earn by work at the job of his choice. Everyone should have the protection of the law and the right to buy and sell. No one could be subjected to physical punishment, to imprisonment without trial or to conscription over his conscientious objections.

A year and a half later Wells wrote that there would be no revolutionary changes in the British social structure because of the war. There would be none because under duress the changes had already taken place. The classless society was, perforce, a reality. He pled again for equal education for everyone.

He was continuing his own formal education. In 1942, when he was seventy-six years old, H. G. Wells took his doctorate in science at London University. His doctoral thesis was "Quality of Illusion in the Continuity of the Individual Life in the Higher Metazoa, with particular reference to *Homo Sapiens*." Man, Wells said in this thesis, was degenerate because he presented no collective resistance in the face of change.

Wells's sons were married now and in homes of their

own. He watched the progress of the war from his Nash Terrace flat. Every day when the weather was not too severe he walked about a mile through war-stricken London. Some days he walked to the Zoo or to Queen Mary's Rose Garden or to the Savile Club. On other days he walked in the opposite direction to Smith's Bookshop on Baker Street. Wells did not make these journeys without difficulty. In his late seventies, his body was beginning to fail his vigorous mind.

He grew bitter as he watched the nations trying to destroy each other. In *'42 to '44* he described Charles de Gaulle as an adventurer and compared him with Hitler. Saying that the Free French general was a *poseur* with a dull military mind who had always grabbed at personal power, he urged England to repudiate him and all he stood for.

When the United States dropped the atom bomb on Hiroshima, August 6, 1945, the atom bomb he had prophesied years before, Wells said, "This can wipe out everything bad—or good—in the world. It is up to the people to decide which."

He seemed to grow even more bitter about his early deprivations. He had been born astigmatic, but no one had paid any attention to his eyes because he was "a common child." He had been undernourished. He had been tubercular. He had been generally underprivileged. Like many others, Wells would have liked to have been born the son of a lord. He had seen early the contrast between Atlas House and Up Park.

Wells said that he had not known normal health until

he was in his thirties. He was suffering now from diabetes and from fatty degeneration of the heart from which both his father and his oldest brother had died.

In 1945 H. G. Wells published the last of his books. They had buoyed him for many years, but now his optimism and his belief in human progress were gone. He had only to look about him to see how badly he had failed. He had failed, and the world had failed. In *Mind at the End of Its Tether* he gave it up.

In his opening paragraphs he said he had tried to bring together in essays, pamphlets, and books "material bearing on the fundamental nature of life and time." He had finished writing now. He was through and civilization was through. He said that there had been a decisive change in life. Man was unable to keep up. He was unable to adapt himself to changed conditions. He could not advance. There was no longer hope for man.

> The end of everything we call life is close at hand and cannot be evaded. . . . The writer is convinced that there is no way out or round or through the impasse. It is the end.

As he had done in *A Modern Utopia* forty years before, Wells quoted Henley's "Invictus." He knew he was nearing his end, but he was still indomitable. He said he was ready to die but continued to watch mankind, "keen to find a helpful use for his accumulations of experience in this time of mental confusion," but he was not hopeful.

Distance had been abolished. Events were practically simultaneous. All was chaos and confusion. There was no pattern to existence. Man could no longer keep pace. He would have to give place to some other animal better adapted to the changes man could neither understand nor meet. Ordinary man was at the end of his tether.

Wells was no ordinary man. His interest in life was undiminished, and the fire was still in him. In 1946 he warned the English royal family to get out before it was thrown out. He said that Churchill too, whom he had previously admired, must go. When a friend tried to get a word into a conversation which, as usual, had become a Wellsian monologue, he would have none of it. "Don't interrupt me! Can't you see I'm dying?"

The New York Times gave Herbert George Wells front-page space on August 14, 1946. His death was announced in two part columns on page one, and his life and accomplishments were reviewed on almost half a page inside the issue. A man of importance and achievement on both sides of the Atlantic was dead. In an article on Sunday, August 25, the *Times* called H. G. Wells "the greatest public teacher of his time."

Just before his death Wells is said to have looked once more at the turmoil and confusion of the world about him and to have exclaimed furiously, "I told you so!"

15

Much of the life of H. G. Wells was a prolonged and enlarged adolescence. The statement and even the words are Wells's from his autobiography.

There is an electric and arresting immaturity about Wells. He had no sense of the slowly accumulated wisdom of the race. Nothing of import had really happened until H. G. Wells came along to explain it, to right the mistakes that had been made, and to insure against any that might be made. In some ways uninformed, in many other ways better informed than most, he was highly intelligent, and consistently demanding. He was youth to the end. That is perhaps the most valuable thing about him.

His youthful energy never diminished. His idealism never faltered. The world never paid him all the attention he felt he deserved, and this annoyed him. Again he is youth. Except in *Kipps* and *Mr. Polly* and in parts of *Tono-Bungay*, he seems light without warmth, brightness without wisdom. He often seems brittle, excited and exciting but unsatisfying.

All that, of course, is only part of it.

Wells was often triumphantly right, not only in prophecy but also in his sensible appraisal of the obvious. When he complained that others did not see and understand and decide correctly and with his own sureness, he was often right too. He was impatient of lesser and slower intellects and of all those too obtuse to agree with him. He wanted only to remake the world and the people in it, and he did not want incompetents getting in his way.

He was a man of action, but he was a writer so the action gushed out in a torrent of words. He had no time for dreaming, no patience with the mystical or the artistic. He cut through love to sex and reveled in its force. The villains in his piece were always conventional restrictions, political ineptitude, unthinking nationalism, and social privileges.

Wells was against many things. Basically he was for just one thing: the world state run along scientific and socialistic lines. When he added his early training in science to his Fabian and post-Fabian socialism, the sum came out to much more than two. It came out to a new-ordered and shining utopia with everyone educated and living a full life. Canby called Wells a "superjournalist." He was, but he was a superjournalist touting for a superscientific civilization in a super- and supranational state.

Where most men forget them or dismiss them in the press of living and working for a living, Wells clung to the ideas and ideals of his youth. He called himself a journalist, and he was in his preoccupation with the contemporary, but he had not the objectivity of the reporter. Despite the year under Huxley, in which he gloried, and the rest of his early study of the sciences, Wells shows little of the scientific attitude and approach. He was emotionally convinced from the beginning that all he believed was objectively true. There was always as much compelling imagination as fierce logic in H. G. Wells.

Wells sped through space like a blazing meteor. He outstripped time. He lived full-bloodedly in his own day. He ranged prehistory, but he dwelt most happily in the future. There seems nothing grotesque in imagining that he might be able to see the world as it is today.

Could H. G. Wells return to see the world he left less than a quarter-century ago he might well congratulate himself on the accuracy of many of his prophecies. He was far too correct when in 1914 he foresaw the atom bomb and its destructive properties. Just as he predicted in *Anticipations,* he would find that trucks roaring over superhighways have largely replaced railroads for the transport of materials and merchandise. He would find people racing about in automobiles on a far greater scale than he had imagined. He would find the airplane an even more common method of travel than he had seen it become.

Wells would find that, just as he predicted, the populations of cities have been dispersed into the suburbs, then more suburbs, then into the countryside beyond the suburbs. He would find that industrial, commercial, and other organized activities have left cities for countryside locations. Wells would hoot his derision at the billions of dollars being poured into "urban renewal" in the United States. Cities have lost their usefulness and much of their economic reason for being. Their reconstruction as historic monuments to an outmoded past would seem to him impractical and ridiculous.

Wells would feel that more progress had been made politically on the pattern he demanded. Both England and the United States have been socialized. Government exerts far greater control over business and individual life. Personal freedom has been deeply curtailed.

There is far greater opportunity for education for everyone. Though it has not yet been made compulsory, college is available to most in the United States. If it is not always free, as he asked in *A Modern Utopia*, scholarships, grants, government subsidies, and the like exist in profusion. Higher education has been made obligatory not just for the capable but is increasingly demanded for the less able. Graduate schooling stands now about where undergraduate schooling stood when Wells wrote his last book.

Whether Wells would approve the huge elementary and secondary educational establishment that has been built up in the United States since World War II is doubtful. With his distrust of professional educators, he might not particularly care for the entrenched and swelling bureaucracy of educational administrators and advisers. His distrust of politicians would make him question sharply the vast expenditures for new buildings and pedagogical schemes and the confused operation of the public educational system.

Wells would welcome the inclusion of more and more practical subjects in school curricula. He might be glad to see American schools used, as they are used, for the palliation of social injustices and as a weapon in racial warfare. It is more likely that he would question the quality of the teachers and the teaching and the effective- ness of the schools in preparing their students for life.

Wells would be horrified at the failure of his most cherished plan. He would be surprised, if not aghast, at the continually worsening international situation.

Instead of disappearing, as he hoped that it would and until his last years felt that it would, violent nationalism flares more fiercely than ever.

Bellicose and threatening, nationalistic sentiment burns hotter every day. Wells's "war to end war" has been followed by a series of greater or lesser armed conflicts. Hot, cold, tepid, declared or undeclared, but always murderous, war has become the accepted order of the day. Instead of a world state, unified, orderly, and operating for the common good, he would find more nations than existed when he lived and all of them intent on advantage at the disadvantage of another. He would find the world engaged in an arms race which dwarfs to insignificance the concerns which he heard discussed at the Washington Disarmament Conference of 1921.

H. G. Wells saw the emergence of the United States and of Soviet Russia as major powers whose attitudes and actions might well determine the fate of all the world. He tried ineffectually to bring about some understanding between them. He would find both nations even more powerful than he had envisioned and with their ideological enmity many times multiplied. Wells would find his utopian world state viciously split on the seemingly opposed concepts of "democracy" and "communism," both operating in an atmosphere of intense mutual hatred and suspicion. He might well exclaim again, "I told you so!"

Could he see what the intervening years have wrought, Wells might even be horrified at the success of some of his utopian socialistic ideas. He would find England a welfare state and riots, bloodshed, arson, and murder deplored in some quarters but rife and flourishing in the United States.

Wells would find the classless society he so strongly advocated an actuality or a near actuality in many places, but he would not find his Samurai, either as a caste or as a permeating attitude anywhere. Nobility is out of fashion.

Wells fought conventional moral standards. He argued against prevailing concepts of the sacredness of marriage and the home and acted on his beliefs. He would approve the "new morality," the sexual freedom, and the general permissiveness in personal behavior applauded today. He had always advocated birth control. He would be glad to see that even where it was once outlawed it is now preached and even advertised by government. In Communist China "Correct Thinking"—the rule book of the state—includes the practice of birth control. It is propagandized in books, films, lectures, even in comic books.

Wells would approve the "new morality," but he would probably deplore and attack youthful withdrawal from the world through drugs, "love," or a sense of the futility of participation. His own reaction to an earlier world he never made either was not defeatism but rebellion and a strong try at accomplishing improvement.

Wells preached the world state from every pulpit he could command, but he was English to the core. At one time he was an enthusiastic imperialist. He propagandized extravagantly for England during World War I. He foresaw the disintegration of the British Empire, but it probably never occurred to him that England would be other than a leader in his utopia. England's was the empire on which the sun never set. Britannia ruled the waves. For generations the world was at peace courtesy of the *Pax Britannica*. The tight little island, the emerald set in a silver sea, was an enduring reality.

Even though Wells saw the bitter aftermath of two world conflicts, even though he had pointed out and underlined her faults for so long, he could hardly have foreseen the rapid decline of his country. It would hurt him to see England reduced to the rank of a third or fourth-rate power—if she is a power at all— and teetering chronically on the verge of bankruptcy.

The United Nations was chartered in San Francisco in 1945. It was a hopeful indication, but Wells would certainly be as impatient with the United Nations as he became with the ineffectual League of Nations. In sympathy with its original aspirations, he would probably condemn it as a mere forum for expressing the extreme nationalistic views of its member nations. Wells had debated tirelessly when he was a student in London. He would ask more than endless debate of what he hoped could be an association of nations in an international body politic.

If before he died Wells was disillusioned with the world

H. G. Wells at about age seventy.

and with the effectiveness of what he considered his role in it, he would find little twenty-five years or so later to ease his despair.

On principle Wells disapproved the reading of novels merely for entertainment. He would disapprove television for the same reason. Yet he might well take some satisfaction in finding that his *Invisible Man* is still known, that Martian invasions are talked about, that children still picture men from outer space much as he described them. He could take serious satisfaction that the space which captured his youthful imagination is now being explored —but not that men are reaching for the moon in a contest for national supremacy in space.

Wells would be humanly pleased that *Kipps* is still read sympathetically, and that *Tono-Bungay* is still accepted as a recognizable picture—from the socialist viewpoint— of the industrial-commercial society of the time it depicts. After more than a half-century, some of his polemical novels are still read because they are strewn with provocative ideas. Wells could be pleased that ever since its publication *The History of Mr. Polly* has been read with delight.

"Swinging London" and the fact that ordinary people hardly dare venture abroad at night on the streets of most American cities might well puzzle H. G. Wells. He had commented as early as 1906 on the prevalence of crime in the United States but could not have realized that it would wax instead of wane. It was part of his naïveté— perhaps the naïveté of his generation—that he assumed decency in human impulse and action. It would puzzle him further that crimes of violence often go unpunished now because society seems unsure whether murder, mugging, and vandalism are crimes, or just expressions of discontent, or the exuberance of their perpetrators, if seldom that of their victims.

Eager, aggressive, a little breathless, H. G. Wells plumped for total world perfection with all the force of his strong mind and his vigorous temperament. His very strenuousness blinded him to other forces.

His own almost instinctive love of England, castigate her as he might and did, should have taught him that men do not easily forswear national loyalties. They will not readily renounce unthinking love of England, France, Kenya, Korea, Vietnam, the United States or any other land to which they are native. They will not transfer allegiance with patriotic fervor to some cold idea which has no reality for them.

Men do not feel and bleed for a theoretical outline. A man may approve Wells's concept of a world state, but he loves a field, a wood, a river, his own street, his home, perhaps even the sky above them. His heart beats to the rhythm of his own place. His body and mind respond to his familiar environment.

Had Wells been a better psychologist, he would have known this. He would also have known that men wish leaders of their own kind. They follow a king, a kaiser, a *duce*, a dictator or a president. They would find it hard to follow the kind of super-technocrats Wells seems to have envisioned. Paying taxes to a world government which has about the personality of a computer would not increase international morale.

Perhaps Wells was too logical, too factual, too rational. Most men are less intellectually motivated. They are less logical, and what they can understand, at least can live in, is a warmer and less reasonable world. Most men are not emotionally affected by chemical formulas or interplanetary ordinances.

Shakespeare did not want a world state. He showed that Romeo and Juliet were in love, that Hamlet was troubled, that Jaques was happy in the Forest of Arden, and that King Lear was betrayed by his daughters. Shakespeare may have lived in simpler times—though no time is simple to those living in it—but More had postulated his utopia a hundred years before Shakespeare, and Bacon's utopian vision appeared at about the same time as Macbeth. Utopian ideas, no matter how logical or how idealistic, do not matter in the face of love, hate, loyalty, jealousy, and the other gripping human emotions. The world state is too impersonal. There is no blood in it. It may well come, but, except as an alternative to certain annihilation, probably not until it is an emotional as well as a logical necessity.

H. G. Wells was seldom stupid. He was always stimulating. He had his limitations, but he lived for all the life that was in him. He took what he could take, and he said what he pleased when he pleased and where he pleased. He looked at life and time and space and he tried hard to make sense of them all. Of course he failed. He undertook what a less driven and more sensible man might sensibly have avoided, but he tried hard and he apologized to no one.

In the end, he had no illusions about himself, his work,

or the world. A lot of what he had written he was willing to discard long before he died. It had served its purpose. For all of him, it could go down the laboratory drain. He was going into the discard too. So—and this hurt him a little—was civilization as he knew it and we know it. Man himself was finished.

Whether Herbert George Wells was right or wrong in his final prophecy remains to be seen.

HERBERT GEORGE WELLS

1866   Born September 21, Bromley, Kent.

1874–1880   Student, Bromley Academy.

1880   Apprenticed to draper, Windsor.
       Pupil teacher, school in Wookey, Somersetshire.

1881   Apprenticed to pharmaceutical chemist, Midhurst.

1881–1883   Apprenticed to draper, Southsea.

1883–1884   Student Assistant, Midhurst Grammar School.

1884–1887   Student, Normal School of Science, London.

1887   Teacher, Holt Academy, Wrexham.

1888   Return to London.

1889–1890   Teacher, Henley House, London.

1891   Marriage to Isabel Mary Wells.

1890–1893   Tutor, University Correspondence College, London.

1895   *The Time Machine*
       Marriage to Amy Catherine Robbins.

1896   *The Island of Dr. Moreau*

1897   *The Invisible Man*

1898   *The War of the Worlds*

1900   Built Spade House
       Love and Mr. Lewisham

1901	*The First Men in the Moon*
1902	*Anticipations*
1903	Joined Fabian Society.
	Mankind in the Making
1905	*Kipps*
	A Modern Utopia
1906	*The Future in America*
	The Faults with the Fabians
1908	Resigns from Fabian Society.
	The War in the Air
1909	*Ann Veronica*
	Tono-Bungay
	Removal to Hampstead Heath.
1910	*The History of Mr. Polly*
1911	*The New Machiavelli*
1914	Visit to Russia
1914–1918	World War I Journalism.
1916	*Mr. Britling Sees It Through*
1918	Worked in Ministry of Propaganda.
	Joan and Peter
1920	Visit to U.S.S.R.
	The Outline of History
1921	Visit to the United States.
1923	*Men Like Gods*
1926	*The World of William Clissold*
1930	*The Autocracy of Mr. Parham*
1933	Visit to the United States.
1934	Visit to U.S.S.R.
	Experiment in Autobiography
1940	*The New World Order*
1945	*Mind at the End of Its Tether*
1946	Died August 14, London.

BIOGRAPHICAL NOTE

As any biography of H. G. Wells must be, this book is based on *H. G. Wells*, the official biography by Geoffrey West (real name G. H. Wells but not related to the book's subject), 1930, the voluminous *Experiment in Autobiography*, 1934, and the other writings of the prolific H. G. Wells. *The Works of H. G. Wells*, Atlantic Edition, 28 vols. (New York: Charles Scribner's Sons, 1924–1927), does not, of course, include the many books which Wells published after that time. Most of the principal Wells books are available in scattered editions issued by various English and American publishers in public libraries and in second-hand bookshops. A number of the scientific romances have been issued in paperback.

These other books proved helpful in the writing of this one:

Bergonzi, Bernard. *The Early H. G. Wells*, a Study of the Scientific Romances. Manchester: The University Press, 1961.

Brooks, Van Wyck. *The World of H. G. Wells*. New York: Mitchell Kennerley, 1915.

Edel, Leon and N. R. Gordon, eds. *Henry James and H. G. Wells*, a Record of Their Friendship, Their Debate on the Art of Fiction, and Their Quarrel. Urbana, Ill.: University of Illinois Press, 1958.

Ervine, St. John G. *Some Impressions of My Elders*. New York: The Macmillan Company, 1922.

Jackson, Holbrook. *The Eighteen Nineties*. New York: Alfred A. Knopf, Inc., 1922.

Jerrold, Douglas. *Georgian Adventure*. New York: Charles Scribner's Sons, 1938.

Raknem, Ingvald. *H. G. Wells and His Critics*. London: George Allen & Unwin, Ltd., 1962.

Swinnerton, Frank. *The Georgian Literary Scene*. London: J. M. Dent, 1938.

Wagar, W. Warren. *H. G. Wells and the World State*. New Haven: Yale University Press, 1961.

Wells, H. G., ed. *Journalism and Prophecy*, 1893–1946. Boston: Houghton Mifflin Co., 1964.